THE
VICTORY
OVER DEATH

—•❖❖❖•—

Episode 4: The Declaration to Eve

JAMES DE ROUSSEAU

Ordering Information:

Prime Seven Media
518 Landmann St.
Tomah City, WI 54660

Printed in the United States of America

*E*lijah Said: Eve I am declaring to you the beginning of the end which has not been done with the WORD with me to do all that will please thee when I speak to CHRIST for him to come and create Spirits in kingdoms for salvation from your flesh in every Nation on earth. I will execute judgment on spirits of gods on the days of salvation CHRIST cast out from your flesh that is Anti CHRIST and has no faith in me, so the Spirits He creates in Kingdoms worthy for salvation can glory until they depart to join you and CHRIST in heaven.

Eve said: Elijah; in the time of salvation will spirits of gods care to know the truth? They will listen to preachers telling stories about devils, gods, and demons to put fear in them to worship God to Death and not CHRIST.

Elijah said: Eve you will be on earth to observe these things before you are dead, and when you are a SPIRIT you will see judgment on spirits removed from the earth and mankind and Israelites populate Kingdoms for salvation

Eve said: O Elijah I look for the day when I depart in the Spirit from this body to be with CHRIST on the throne in heaven.

Elijah said: Eve after you depart from your body you shall continue on earth to observe everything on earth until you resurrect to the throne to see final judgment by the WORD, while spirits of gods are in your flesh the peace on earth is delayed.

Eve said: Elijah, it was a terrible sin that Satan did to rape me to make a god to die to face Death. Elijah answered, that is why CHRIST created me to save spirits that has faith in me from falling to Death to rest in Peace when salvation begin. Eve said: Elijah how long will I have to stay on earth after my body is dead. I am suffering in this body for making a god (cain)

Elijah said: Zion You are suffering, CHRIST is suffering, both of you created to live together, He is on the throne in heaven and you are still manifest in your image in His flesh with stress, torment and humiliated on earth. Flesh has no heavenly existence. You made a god and saw paradise loss without your Sons and daughters to populate on earth while you are in your image.

But when you will be in the Spirit without flesh you will be in heaven to see Paradise regain with Spirits of creation populating the earth in righteousness in your flesh until they depart and join you and CHRIST on your throne in heaven.

Elijah said: Zion do you understand the problem Satan the and the other devils have left on earth with spirits from there seed of Death in your flesh? The spirits of gods will blame you and not the devils for raping you to make a god to pass on the seed of Death to make gods to destroy flesh with disease of Death.

The gods will preach to gods, Eve is a sinner but will not say it is devils who sinned, other preachers will say it is Adam that sin through disobedience and not the devils. They will not preach the devils raped all your Daughters to make gods and giants. They will be afraid to say Judah hanged the body of CHRIST and killed all Your Sons to make mankind and Israelites after the devils was removed from the earth.

Elijah said: Zion while you are manifest in your image as Eve you will be deprived of heavenly privilege and live among the accursed spirits until you resurrect to heaven to sit next to CHRIST in dignity to see Righteous Judgment on spirits that is anti CHRIST and have no Faith for Peace.

While you are on earth you will see spirits multiply Kingdoms with spirits born in sin until the hour come for you to ask them to have mercy, and to forgive them for being born in your flesh through rape by devils and to have faith for salvation for their kingdoms, For CHRIST to create Spirits by the WORD to continue in their images to populate the earth in righteousness with no faults to join you and CHRIST on HIS throne in heaven.

Elijah said: Zion this Peace on earth is through sacrifice and patience to populate Spirits according to the New Testament for all Spirits created to be righteous and equal to live in peace and harmony to enjoy the prosperity with eternal Life to make the covenant with statutes with devils obsolete.

The New Testament is to make a clean sweep in the kingdom to eliminate godly spirits born in sin to the last seed. CHRIST said vengeance is mine an eye for an eye he will repay and remove the spirits of devils for spilling his blood on earth.

KING JUDAH (Ps;51.3)

King Judah became popular, out of respect the gods called him mighty God, he boasted he created Israelites and mankind and god in Hades killed one holy One, but King Judah has killed thousands from Adam to be a creator, He boasted what the devils did King Judah can do and build Babylon for all on earth to live by his law, he would drink and get drunk and kill who did not worship him, He was angry because he was born in sin and not accepted in Heaven and had a choice to have eternal Peace.

THE BEGINNING OF MANKIND AND ISRAELITES

Eve became a nursemaid to the baby gods and giant babies from her dead daughters and supervised to see the godly women breastfed the baby gods and kept them clean. Judah became the god father of giant baby gods of the dead daughters of Eve.

The godly queens of the devils sold some giant babies to merchants to propagate with their gods and mankind began to have different features from gods

Judah betroth his mother (Tamuze) kept her in captivity. Tamuze became the queen of Babylon and the children he had with his mother he called Israelites as his creation. He gave his commandant and soldiers baby gods and sold some he did not select to mix with his Israelites to populate his creation.

THE HAREM

The godly women in the harem taught the first born of the dead daughters of Eve how to give pleasure to King Judah to get pregnant to make mankind babies for the king this caused much jealousy and fighting in the harem.

The maidens who was not pregnant for Judah had priority and was massaged with oil to stimulate them to be pregnant, those who were pregnant were jealous of Virgins that would be next to have the kings pleasure to be pregnant to make mankind babies. All the children of the dead daughters of Eve became pregnant for Judah and died giving birth.

THE FUN ROOM

The Maidens he did not select that survived the birth and could not be pregnant for Judah, he invited his friends to participate in abomination, and they did like the devils and put on masks of dogs, falcon, black panther to fuck like creatures of the earth. Then the maidens would be sold to priests, commandants and tribal gods to populate different features. Eve and the godly women brought up all his children in the harem to mix with his Israelites in the palace to populate.

Queen Tamuze had no idea what Judah was doing to satisfy his insatiable lust, he would whip his daughters to satisfy him, but there was one of his daughters he could not have enough, her name is Haddasah, neither she could have enough of him, she had a son by him she called Belhadasah, Judah got jealous she spent too much time with her Bel and gave him to a witch doctor to adopt.

In the palace, Judah said: Tamuze Elijah is not interested in spirits that has no faith in Him he look at spirits of gods as shit in the kingdom. You are my Queen and I should have rights over kingdoms from your flesh and not Elijah.

Queen Tamuze said: What is the big deal, you can have the spirits from your seed in the gate as Elijah promised you before you took the Law under oath. What Elijah does with kingdoms from my flesh of my Father has nothing to do with you.

When the time come, CHRIST will cast out godly spirits from my Flesh, for Elijah to judge who has no faith in him like you, to return your spirits to you in the gate as he promised you, you have condemned yourself by hanging the body of my Father and killing all my brothers like god (Cain) who raped me. (Dan 2.47:Eph 4.24)

Judah said: I hate Elijah in the image of god in the kingdom. I am a king of all nations on earth and all gods obey me. Only you and your Mother are left on earth until the gods condemn the both of you for making them not holy to be accepted above.

Tamuze said: Then it will be justified For CHRIST and ELIJAH to remove all godly spirits from the earth from the day they pass judgment on my Mother and me. They will be doing the same as you eliminating holy people from the earth. You put your hope in the law to keep me in captivity to commit sin to make Israelits.

You are doing the same as the devils who held me captivity to make gods and not wanting me to see my Mother who is innocent like me of sin. Elijah will give us Holy Spirits in Kingdoms from our flesh through CHRIST. And we will see you perish in the final judgment with the devils to Death.

Judah said: Tamuze, You committed abomination with the devils to make gods to be sinners, you are a witch burdened with sin of devils, if I don't kill you gods, mankind and Israelites will for making them on earth with hate and malice of devils and not accepted above.

THE WARNING

Judah had a dream: Elijah said my Judgment is not like you think, neither my way is like your way, for as heaven is higher than the earth, so is my way higher than your way that lead to Death. Every god that has no respect for the Judge of the whole earth or the Queen of the universe or the Queen of the earth shall fall and return to face Death according to the New Testament because of ignorance and having no Faith in me.

In Fear after this Vision and warning Judah said: Tamuze you are not allowed in the harem to see Eve or even talk with her. Tamuze replied you are like a dragon for my flesh and want to dominate me in the palace I have to endure all your deceit for peace. As a king you should use this opportunity to do good for the gods, what profit is it if you populate the earth with spirits of gods and Israelites and after they are dead to fight with you against Elijah to perish to Death.

Tamuze went on to say: You fuck with the children from my dead sisters to create mankind with your Israelites from your seed to provoke Elijah. He will return there spirits to you in the gate in the final judgment? My flesh is my inheritance on earth.

Judah said: I am the king of the earth and my plan is to populate spirits from my seed to fight with me against Elijah for the earth until there is no flesh left from you or your Mother to inherit on earth. The loss of kingdoms from your flesh will be through my wickedness to be the king of the spirits of the earth, I am not like you, when you are a Spirit your Faith in Elijah to live forever the eternal life above.

Tamuze said: All godly spirits will be like rubbish without my flesh and will be swept clean like dust from the earth to face the devils and Death in the everlasting fire because of your laws, the godly spirits will pluck out your eyes for making them on earth to fight your wars and spill blood to be a king of the spirits with false doctrine of devils to leading many astray with your imagination (MT 4.8 Lk12.32 Gen6.4-5) as your creation with innocent women in captivity you abused to satisfy your lust.

My Father told me all what I am telling you will happen before I was kidnapped by devils. My Father said: Elijah is the only one I should trust, so think twice of this plan to make war to destroy holy flesh on earth, gods can worship you but my Flesh is for Elijah to give me children that is pleasant, he is patient with you he is the a King of Peace and not War. One WORD from his mouth and you will perish like the devils for your wickedness.

THE TEN COMMANMENTS

Judah held Tamuze in his arms and carried her to the bed, Tamuze cried you are forcing me again to commit more sin. to your sin, you are worse than Satan, you are a god you must not have sex with holy people it is trespass its not allowed, to make a god to hate holy people

Judah with inflamed passion forcing her, she slapped his face said stop it, he grinned, I am your king Ill commit this ten commandments with you while I am in your flesh, as long as I live I will make Israelites with you.

Tamuze began to cry, you are a tyrant with your vanity and boasting you are a creator and fornicating with hate to make me pregnant. Your bones will stick out for this sin to bring another like you on earth full of wickedness to live by the law. There will be no hope for the spirits from you born in sin by transgression.

Judah said: By my power you will live under the law as my queen in Babylon and not under the oath of devils to make gods under oath. You will make Israelites for your king as long as I live in this body.

Tamuze said: you are a foolish King like the devils, they taught they could live on earth forever, they made you corrupt, boastful and you imitate them, you have become a king in your imagination, wicked and abominable with lust abusing me in captivity forcing me to live under your laws, I was born free from laws. Elijah will be our Judge.

Judah held her by her throat and said: I will kill you if you dont submit willingly you will be punished by your King when I am dead you will be free. Tamuze shouted you fucking bastard Elijah will punish you after you are dead and it will be justified for your abuse and taking advantage of the children of dead holy women to make mankind. (1Tim 1.7)

Judah was furious she answered back and said: The object of my hate and malice and anger is because you and god (Cain) your brother who was the first to fuck you to make a god as wicked as him, to pass on his accursed seed to make gods to suffer with disease from Death.

Tamuze answered its my flesh you have lust for, why don't you celebate? You are complaining about a rapist god who was the first, you cannot have enough and want to abuse me until you are dead. When your spirit depart from your dead body you will cry when Elijah cast your ass out of the earth to be with devils for making Israelites with his Queen to await judgment for what you have done because of jealousy and provocation to make me pregnant, to passing on the accursed seed to populate the earth to fight against him for the earth.

Judah slapped her face, Tamuze fell on the floor dizzy, she cried, go away from me, you wicked god in conspiracy with devils you did the same as Cain to kidnap me, to hold me in captivity you are wicked like him, Judah shouted it is my wickedness that made me your King.

Tamuze said: I have to endure your fornication in shame for peace, but I will live to see you cry and beg Elijah for peace, and she slammed the door and began to cry O Elijah have pity on me, save me from this tyrant. The voice of Elijah said: When you go to heaven you will see Judgment on all the devils and Judah who has held you and your Mother in captivity. Be patient, and Tamuze fell asleep

Judah was furious, went in the harem held Eve and dashed her head on the wall and said: I blamed you for making god (Cain) to be my father from now you will separated from the Maidens from your dead Daughters to live in your own quarters, he made the godly women and eunuchs servants prepared the virgins for him to make them pregnant to make mankind. The maidens in harem were now teenagers of the dead Daughters of Evewho gave birth to them in the harem.

Judah said to Hadassah and her sisters: you are going to be mother fuckers to make mankind for me I will kill every baby born in the harem that look like god of Eve with Satan, In fear they said we will make Mankind for you o king and you can kill the gods you don't like, He went on his chariot, hit the horses with the rod and went out of the palace to the city to drink and get drunk.

Eve cried night after night Elijah save me and Tamuze from this tyrant, Judah is going to make mankind with the children from my dead daughters and making Israelites with Tamueze in the palace.

Elijah appeared He said: Judah is provoking me sinning with Tamuze and planning to destroy the kingdoms from your flesh so spirits from his seed can fight with him against me for the earth, and destroy all with flesh to prevent you and Tamuze inheriting kingdoms for salvation for CHRIST to create Spirits by the WORD

Now there are gods, Israelites, Giants and Mankind in your flesh making godly spirits in this generation they have done you no harm and its not justified to judge them for the sin of Judah and devils, neither can salvation take effect in kingdoms while you are living in your image, but if mankind, Israelites, gods on earth from the accursed seed of devils harm you or Tamah ask them to have mercy on you and Tamah for being born not Perfect to be accepted above and forgive them for being born in sin with faults of devils, tell them of the choice they have to have Faith to have the eternal peace or fall.

Elijah said: Neither will you have mercy by angels in heaven unless you ask them to have mercy on you for making a god to be the righteous Queen of all worlds in the universe knowing good and evil to be the conqueror of Death.

Elijah said: ZION you asked me to save you and Tamah from the tyrant; Zion while you are in your image you have to observe all what Judah and his Israelites, Mankind, gods and giants do while you live among them in captivity.

So when you are on the throne in heaven to see CHRIST return at the appointed time when the earth is populated to remove spirits of gods from kingdoms to create Spirits in multitudes to continue to populate the earth with Immortal Spirits with everlasting life to be with you and CHRIST forever in the worlds above with no faults.

Zion said. O Elijah I have given you and CHRIST a lot of Work on the days of Salvation. Elijah said this work will be according to the New Testament for all spirits to have a choice to have faith to rest the eternal Peace on earth.

Zion said: Elijah I am old in this body, CHRIST and all my SONS and Daughters are in heaven its only Tamah and I are left on earth with you My Son with the WORD you are my savior I am not afraid what gods will do to me they are only on earth for seasons to make kingdoms, and Tamah and I are on earth humiliated by this tyrant provoking you. Forgive me Elijah for all this work for peace on earth.

Elijah said: Zion be patient, when you and CHRIST are on the throne in heaven you will be conquerors of the worlds in the universe with beautiful people on the earth living the long life like you until they they are in the heavens for ever joining you and CHRIST living the everlasting life in prosperity in worlds without end.

Eve said: after much suffering and humiliation I will have peace. Elijah Ill be patient to receive the good from the earth for my suffering. Elijah said: with much patience the farmer cultivate to produce much quality fruit for your suffering and you shall not be ashamed you made a god in your youth to remind you of sin and you will be happy with what CHRIST will give you with no pain and sorrow. Elijah disappeared after comforting Zion and told her to be patient to receive the best of the earth.

KING JUDAH OF BABYLON

Judah concentrated to build Babylon to be the greatest city as the commerce center of the earth, his nation was populating more and more, set up schools for Pharisees to teach the law for all on earth to worship him as their creator, out of respect. They worship him as the almighty God.

Tamuze said: Judah now everyone is worshiping you as a mighty God use this opportunity to do good for all on earth, what will you gain if you populate the earth with spirits of gods in and Israelites to fight against Elijah. They will perish like the devils in the tornado and will not return to earth.

You are fucking the maidens from my dead sisters to create mankind for Israelites to fuck, to populate Israelites to be kings to rule the other nations with godly kings what you are doing will create jealousy and hate.

Judah said: I am a King. The God of Israelites and they should fight to be kings to rule nations with me and to populate multitudes on earth to live by my law to have control in the nations that is my plan. They must worship and have respect for me, your flesh is not important if they die they will be spirits it is through my wickedness they are Kings to live by my laws. I am not like you I have a spirit of a god that has no faith Your Spirit live forever.

Tamuze said to Judah all godly spirits in my flesh will be like the rubbish of the earth if they don't have faith and live by your laws, they will be awful like you and wish they had a place to live and rest in peace when they die, they will enter humans and seduce them to lead spirits of mankind to fall through ignorance of the truth and false worship. (Gen 6 4-6.)

She Said to Judah Satan and the other devils will chain you with the king of devils for making mankind with their gods while they are in the heat and making Israelites in the palace. Death Said to the devils he want all spirits that pass on his seed to return to him because he is the father of Sin and disease. So think twice about your plan. My Father told me before I was kidnapped by Satan all what is happening in this generation Tamuze felt sorry for him.

EPISODE 4

The Ten Commandments

*J*udah held Tamuze in his arms and carried her to the bed. Tamuze cried you are forcing me again to have sex to add to your sin. You are a god you are trespassing in holly flesh again to make another like you with Hate for holy people. Judah inflamed with passion pushed her on the bed, she slapped his face, stop it she shouted, he grinned I am going to commit the covenants of Death with you. As long as I live on earth you will be my queen to live under the law. By my power ill set you Free from the oath of devils and do as I say as my Queen.

JUDAH KING OF BABY LON

Judah concentrated to build Babylon to be the greatest city on earth to be the commerce center on earth. His nation was populating more and more. He built a new palace for queen Tamuze, set up schools for Pharisees to teach the law to mankind to worship him as the Mighty God who created them to live to Death.

THE CONNECTION OF THE BEGINNING (GEN.1.12)

The godly queens began to get jealous there kings was making the daughters of the dead holy daughters in there harem pregnant. As soon as they gave birth they were sold to rulers of tribes and merchants to mix with their gods to make mankind with different features from gods of devils.

ELIJAH TOOK A REST (MT 27.1; HEB11.10-13;PS118.19.26)

The behaviour of Judah the adopted son of Elijah he called Ammon has brought problems to Christ and his family on earth, Ammon is subject to violence, conspiracy, and deceit of devils. He kept Tamuze in captivity to make children with his mother and children with her dead sisters and kept Eve in captivity, his plan is for the spirits from his seed in kingdoms to populate spirits in the nations to be godly spirits to make war against Elijah for the Earth.

Elijah is merciful and has no pleasure in Judah,s death and has taken this threat of war for the earth seriously and give him extra time while he is a spirit in his humanity, Judah is disappointed he is not accepted in heaven therefore he is not interested in Salvation to rest in peace would rather take a chance and fight against Elijah for the earth. Judah is a jealous god, his mother is accepted in heaven but not him, Elijah will save his mother but not him, he has condemned himself for hanging the body of ADAM/CHRIST on a tree and killing 1440000 of the Sons of CHRIST with much hatred for holy people on earth.

Elijah withdrew himself from the provocation of Amon/Judah knowing if he spoke one WORD where Judah spirit will end. Judah kept piling on the pressure humiliating Eve and Tamuze, He know Elijah is slow when it comes to anger and very patience as a father to an adopted son.

Elijah took a break and rested, Eve and Tamuze did not know where he abode or heard from him or what became of him. Fear and trembling was on Eve and Tamuze living under the power of a tyrant, all they had was Faith in Elijah to save them.

Elijah is the Master builder with a plan of CHRIST to do the work according to the New Testament in the ark in the tabernacle the ETERNAL prophesied all what CHRIST will do if the devils made a god with HIS creation on Earth. That his CHRIST will create his ELIJAH that is more powerful than any devil or god to rule all on earth and HIS CHRIST rule in the the Kingdoms on earth and have dominion in all worlds in the universe and creator Spirits in Kingdoms from his flesh. CHRIST said to Elijah Salvation is far off, an eye for an eye, when I Return on Earth ill take vengeance in the kingdoms on earth.

THE gods of the devils began to blame mankind, Israelites, and Giants for taking over the earth and wanted the devils to return to save them from Judah

Judah went to the harem and saw Eve crying, she said you have made the maiden from my dead daughters pregnant to humiliate me. Judah said: for this purpose I adopted them to create mankind to look different from gods

Judah went back to the palace told Tamuze your Mother is crying because your dead Sisters children are pregnant for me. Tamuze said can Igo and see my Mother? Judah said no you are not allowed to go to the harem. Tamuze you want me to be an alien to my Mother. You are possessed with a spirit of hate for me and my Mother and went in her room. Judah rushed inside the room with anger and held Tamuze by her throat and said I will kill you if it's the last thing I do on this earth

Tamuze said fucking do it now and you will know who will come after you, I am pregnant like a cow full of your bitterness and hate to fight your war.

Judah ran outside the palace knowing if he put his hand on her he would kill her, he put his head in his hands realized he is mad, wanting to cry but tears won't come. He began to say this hate is like a consuming fire burning inside me. I can't be humble to My mother hearing the voice of Elijah in his head from his youth save her from devils but the day you commit abomination with your mother Ill abandon you. Now for the first time he understood to have faith to be My Son in Creation for everlasting Peace.

Babylon city became active with all kinds commerce everywhere people was buying and selling, wherever Judah went the people would bow and worship him as there God who created them. No one spoke of devils they were ancient history.

GIANTS OF ANAK

The giant babies of the raped women by Anak devils were called Anakins Judah trained the Anakins as his warriors to protect his Israelites; they were his elite fighters in the stadium fighting other giants with shield and spear.

The godly kings imitated Judah and trained their giants bred with their gods and called there Giants Gollia. Mankind, gods, Israelites and Giants began to populate the earth with people with different features height and size all nations on earth as is in this generation.

LIFE IN THE PALACE

Tamuze was always pregnant with Israelites running after her with tinkle bells on their feet, running around the palace playing with Siamese cats and rabbits, in the palace garden was a variety of exotic birds singing and making noise, peacocks showing off their plumage when the cats came around them fish ponds with all kinds of coloured fish.

When there was peace between Tamuze and Judah the harp players would play soothing music for Judah to fall asleep, the servants would wash under his feet, clip his toenails and massage his feet with herbal oils and he would fall asleep in peace and snore'

THE TOWER OF BABEL

Judah built the tower of Babel it was the tower in Babylon in the tower was a temple at the top for his body to be after he died, and where the people could worship him and queen Tamuze every full moon.

The second tier of the tower was for his Israelites to occupy on the ceremonies for burnt offerings. The other tiers on the tower was for mankind and rulers of other nations.

The tower of Babel was in the centre of the square where all the people would gather to worship King Judah as Mighty God with Queen Tamuze mother of the Living and the Dead to provoke Elijah.

In front of the tower was a statue in the image of the unknown god (Cain) in Hades for gods to sacrifice godly children as a burnt offering to god in Hades every full moon in front of God and his Queen mother, to provoke Elijah that all on earth worship Him as there Mighty God and not Elijah.

The first day the full moon appeared. The trumpeter went to the top of the tower and blue his horn for the procession to begin, people came from everywhere to the tower of Babel to worship King Judah as there Mighty God who created them and brought gifts for Queen Tamuze.

After the king and Queen sat the trumpeter blew his horn on top of the tower of Babel and everyone began to postulate on the ground to worship King Judah The mighty God of Israelites and mankind and Giants, then they stood and began to say: O mighty God and Queen mother of us all on earth, we worship you Pray to the unknown god for our sins and tell him to save us from devils after we are dead.

They postulated again the horn blower blew the horn, and the people in the square said: O mighty God of Israelites and mankind we worship you, fill the earth from your seed to populate all kinds of image for ever.

The gods postulated and stood, said: O mighty God we worship you with the fear of Death, let there always be bread to eat and water to drink before we return to death.

The chief Pharisee of the Israelites said: O God we are Israelites for posterity to pass on your seed for all generations, God our father we give you praise for building the tower of Babel to come and worship you, and for gods of our mother to sacrifice to the unknown god in Hades as a burnt offering before you and our mother at the tower.

Another Israelite said; O Mighty God rule over us forever and make us Kings to rule nations on earth forever. Then horn blower blew the horn after he was through speaking. The people stood and looked up at the top of the tower where Judah sat with Tamuze his Mother and queen and said: Hail King of Kings God of the unknown god we are ready for the burnt offering of gods to start; Judah put his thumb down and the wood on the altar with statue of the unknown god (Cain) was set alight'

Then the gods began throw their sons and daughters in the flames of wood on the altar to sacrifice as a burnt offerings to the unknown god in Hades to save them and the queen for making them with devils. (Ro 14.22-23;Ro 8 5-9)

THE WASTE OF FLESH
(IS1.10-15 LEV 20.14)

After the sacrificial ceremony Judah and Tamuze went back to the palace, Tamuze said: Judah, too much of my flesh is going to waste, I have no desire to participate in New moon sacrifices to try out your plan to kill gods for (cain) and devils in Hades, you should be the first to sacrifice for your peace with Elijah, you have forgotten you are, a god who has no faith and killing gods to be godly spirits to possess bodies after they are dead to seduce people to be wicked like you. Tamuze said: I do not want to take any part of these new moon sacrifices while Israelites and mankind abide on earth in my flesh. (Ro 14.9-12) Eze45.16-17) Eze.46,1-2) Deut 32.7-17)

Judah got angry and said: you are always complaining you are never satisfied with what I do and held Tamuze by her throat shouting Ill kill you. The Israelite prince rushed at him; don't kill our mother, there was a struggle, one of the princes took the rod and hit Judah on the head and he fell and passes out.

Tamuze ran in the harem to get away from Judah, she met Eve for the first time since she was kidnapped by Satan and was held in captivity, Tamuze said mother Judah tried to kill me he has kept me away from seeing you, I don't want to go back in the palace

EVE AND TAMUZE

Eve said: I am being punished for making a god/ (cain) and you are punished for making gods for Satan who raped me to make a god, the devils have caused much problems for you and I on earth. We are the only two holy people left on earth I feel humiliated living in this place among godly women and pregnant grand children from your dead sisters. My daughter while we live in captivity by this tyrant, all we have is Faith in Elijah to save us.

No matter how much seed mankind, Israelites, gods and Giants pass to populate the earth to make godly spirits; our flesh is our inheritance for salvation for your Father to create New Spirits to live the Everlasting life.

Tamuze said: Mother Cain raped me to make a god for him before I was kidnapped by the devils, I gave birth to his god in the bush to prevent Satan from eating him from birth and asked Elijah to save him; I wish I knew what happened to my first god with Cain. Mother nothing seem to go right for me, I go from one bad situation to another since I was kidnapped by Satan and devils I am held in Captivity

Eve said: You want to know what happened to your god with Cain; my daughter, Judah is your god you left in the bush, Elijah heard your plea to save him from Satan. Now he is your King

Tamuze said: so Judah knew I was his mother. He forced me to have sex with him to add to my shame? I fear Father will be angry with me for making a god. Now I am betroth to a murderer who exterminated all my my Brothers from the earth, and want me to be silent, and be submissive, he gets angry every time I speak, I am ashamed to be making Israelites to be against Elijah and CHRIST my Father

I asked him what he was doing he said he was making mankind to mix with his princes in the palace to speed up population of Israelites to have better features than the gods I made as his creation. I am in fear my Father will be angry with me for making a god to hang his body on a tree to be a king with devils.

Eve said: My daughter I would not like you to be ignorant, Judah is the son of my your god (Cain) he is in Hades for raping you, Elijah heard your god crying in the bush where you gave birth to him and adopted him, taught him scriptures and many skills he had no faith in salvation to create a SPIRIT to be his Son by the WORD for his spirit to rest in the everlasting peace. Elijah said: if he had faith and needed help to save you from the devils all he had to do is call Him.

But when he saw your beautiful face he lusted and took the oath of the devils to be against Elijah and CHRIST.

Tamuze said: If Satan had eaten him from birth I would be free from the oath, now we are living under his law while he is populating the earth with gods, mankind, Israelites and Giants in our flesh what a catastrophe on earth only CHRIST and Elijah can solve this and save us with righteous judgment while we are on earth for making gods through rape

Eve said: my daughter I am old I wish I could help you if you stayed in the harem, Judah will be angry and kill the pregnant women here for him, return to the palace for peace sake and hold on to your faith that Elijah will save us when the time comes for righteous judgment.

Tamuze said; Mother could you come to the palace with me to speak to Judah, all I want is peace in my life from all this drama, hate, envy and wickedness on earth. I hope he can get a godly woman I am ashamed. Eve said: he likes Hadassah in the harem and she cannot have enough of him.

Eve and Tamuze went to the Palace, Eve confronted Judah, you have shed blood of my Sons and now you want to kill your mother who saved your life from devils, you have no love for her, Elijah brought you up after she gave birth to you in the bush to do good but instead you fornicate with your mother and blaspheme Elijah and Christ. And took the oath to be against Elijah and CHRIST

Judah answered; Eve my malice is not against you, She is the object of my rage and hate for conceiving me from the accursed unholy seed in her womb from your god (Cain) and I am now passing on his seed to make Israelites and Mankind with all his faults through me in her flesh. I am not accepted and holy righteous to go above.

Eve said; Elijah gave you a choice so your spirit could rest and have the evelasting sleep in peace, so your body could be for salvation to create a Spirit to be his Son in creation and not from the accursed seed. Your mother was raped by god your father (Cain), so don't take revenge on my daughter for making you unholy to pass on the seed of god/cain of the devil to make Israelites and Mankind with many faults of devils, You keep your mother in captivity like the devils, and prevent me from seeing my daughter to nurse your children with my daughters who died in your captivity after they were raped by devils. Elijah removed the devils from the earth with righteous judgment for rape.

Eve went on to say: we are the only two holy women left on earth and you want to take revenge on us, because you were born in sin, you hold us in captivity with the law of devils that are no more on the face of the earth.

Judah shouted. Tamuze is a whore burdened with sin, I am her King and not a devil that held her in captivity to make gods, Eve you are in captivity as a nurse maid to mankind from my seed

Eve said you are wicked, hanged the body of her Father, Slay all her brothers and hold the both of us in captivity. I am a witness to all you have done, Elijah will take revenge for transgression, your sin is grievous to my daughter. She only endures what you do for peace. I am sorry for you and all spirits from your accursed seed who has no Faith like you for eternal peace and Eve walked back to the harem.

Tamuze began to cry: Why have you done this? You came in my room and saw your mother,s nakedness and fucked me to give me children in abomination to make me a shame in the eyes of Elijah.

Judah said now you know I am your first god I will seduce you and see you naked for leaving me in the bush naked in your blood and denying me the pleasure to suck milk from your breast, now you will worship me forever. I hate you for making me a god to make gods to make kingdoms for salvation from your flesh for their spirits to face Death. Ill destroy your holy flesh to the last drop of blood on earth with spirits from my seed.

Tamuze cried, Elijah was good to you, you allowed the devils to deceive you with their covenant with Death to have authority to rule gods by their law. The devils made you a murderer to be a king of gods in much shame and sorrow I left you in the bush to save you from the devils.

MT 7.6) (ESSEK 25.15) THINK NOT I CAME TO DESTROY YOUR LAW.

Instead of love you hate me for saving you, you hate CHRIST you have not seen in the body of Adam and Elijah who brought you up before you took the law of devils under oath, you make Israelites to live under the oath, and saw me trembling in fear.

I had to endure all what the devils did to my body for peace; you satisfy your lust for making Isrelites and disobeyed Elijah who told you not to fornicate with me, you failed the test on faith.

(2PET 2.4) ELIJAH DID NOT SPARE THE DEVILS

Tamuze said: I am sorrowful with grief, Judah I suffered much under the oath before your face, you are no help to me, instead you add on to my sorrow. You slayed 1440000 of my Brothers with your batalion of gods, I feel unclean with you with the blood of my brothers on your hands, you have no hope with CHRIST and Elijah for what you did to my brothers and to me.

Judah could not stand to hear the truth, he blocked his ears. Stood there steering at Tamuze in shock. Tamuze said; you tried to prevent me from heavenly entry, If you were a wise King you would have accepted the everlasting peace for your spirit for salvation for your kingdom in my flesh to have a Son in Creation to be accepted.

Suddenly when he heard the word salvation he came out of shock and slap Tamuze on her face, she fell she cried I don't need your mercy kill me so I don't see your face another day.

Judah dragged her from the floor and threw her on the bed and began to fuck her saying you will have children for me until you are dead and you will see who is the builder in your flesh for salvation from spirits from my seed.

Tamuze cried you fucking bastard don't slap me kill me, you were born from the wickedness of god your father of Satan, you will meet your match in wickedness. Judah said; I am your King and you will see my face when your Spirit separate from your dead body. He spat in her face for telling him he is of the god of Satan, and put his feet on her throat.

THE FIRST AND LAST WARNING BY ELIJAH (2PET 2.4)

Elijah appeared in the room as he was about to strangle her, Judah looked and in fear said to Elijah: what do you want? Tamuze cried out he was going to kill me, save me from him. Elijah said to

Tamuze: rise from the floor, fear not me, behold, because of your Faith in me, you are in the presence of your Elijah.

WOE (JER23.1) (MK14.58)

Elijah said: Tamuze I have come to warn your god offshoot of Satan on the throne of devils with malice, deceit, hate, jealous while he live in your flesh, he has rebelled against me and CHRIST, and became a destroyer of innocent people who has done him no harm.

Elijah said: Judah in front of your mother, this is my first warning. If you harm your mother, you will be in the chambers prepared for the wicked and you will be with the devils waiting in the final Judgment. Judah began to tremble when he heard he will be with devils.

Elijah said: when you walked with me I called you Ammon. The devils called you Judah. This is my final warning to you, if your mother or her Mother shed one Tear from their eyes by you I will be back, and this time it will be you who will be crying to me to save you from devils you placed your hope after you are dead. (Essek. 16.3)

AMMON THOU HAS MULTIPLIED GODS (GAL 3.18)(ESSEK 16.29)

Elijah said Ammon I have restrained myself from punishing you, I have held my peace. I have been patient with you to take action because you are angry for the way you were born which is no fault of yours, or your mother as well. You were brought up to know scripture and the choice you had for everlasting peace and not to fall in the pit before you took the oath to be a prophet to gods of devils.

NO FAITH (IS 54.16) (GEN 18.22)

Elijah said Ammon the next time you see my face, it will be to pass judgment on you to separate you from your mother,s flesh. Judah said you should destroy her with the wicked devils. Elijah did not answer and vanished.

The both stood there watching each other, it was the first time Tamuze saw Elijah she did as CHRIST her father said the only Elijah she must trust to save you before she was kidnapped by the devils and held in captivity by devils.

DON'T TOUCH WHO IS HOLY (2TIM.3.4)

Judah tried to touch tamuze, she said don't touch me else I cry one tear and you are finished on earth. You heard what your master said to you. And she went to the harem to be with Eve to tell her the good news.

Tamuze suffered in silence, her heart was not with the children she had and looked at them as though they are not hers, she made gods for devils, Israelites for Judah was no big deal, if they have faith they will have everlasting sleep or join Judah in the gate as promised for having no Faith in Elijah.

REJOICE IN YOUR FAITH (1PET 1.26) (1COR 13.6-7.25)

Eve said; Cursed is he who has sex with daughters of my dead daughters to make mankind to have thousands of different features from gods in their flesh, My Daughter you are worthy to have mercy from Elijah. The Kingdoms from their flesh is your inheritance for Elijah to give you perfect children in the time of salvation

Eve said: Judah is the father of all the mankind children in the harem he boast they are his creation to populate the earth from his seed, my Daughter you are good your affliction has taught you to know good and evil on earth, you are worthy to have mercy. These children will face many troubles in there life only their faith in Elijah will save them.

Judah took heed of the WORDS of Elijah and knew one mistake to make Tamuze or Eve cry he would be in the whirlwind to join god (Cain) and the devils in Hades. In fear of Hades, he took his chariot and rode the horses with fierce anger to the camp with his battalion and put his energy to train the giant Anakins he save in the harem to fight with spear and shield until they became fighters.

He trained mankind with his battalion of gods who were with him when he went to slay the Sons of CHRIST in there humanity they became his new soldiers for war to rule the earth as a part of his plan.

O KING OF NATIONS
(JER10.7) (REV 19.19) (REV 3.4)

Judah declared war on the godly kings in the other nations, Judah set up battle formation with his Anakin Giants, mankind and gods with bow and arrow to attack and conquer the nations to eliminate the godly kings of the godly queens of devils. This battle was a trial strategy of Judah,s plan to fight for the earth with godly spirits against Elijah

WAR OR PEACE (ECCL 3.8)

The battalion of mankind on horses followed by worrier Giants and gods beating war drums advancing in the nations of the godly kings. The gods in the nations could here this drumming and saw the battalion of soldiers coming to their nation began to close their door in fear for their life.

The soldiers surrounded the palace, and there was silence, the commandant of the soldiers shouted to the king to come out and surrender your nation in peace to King Judah, or we will come to bring you out to face our King.

The godly king came outside outraged with his officials and said, Judah what is the reason for coming in my nation with your battalion? Judah pulled out his sword from its sheath and cut off the head of the king. The princes came out from the palace and said who gave you the right to kill our king? The gods said to the princes you are insulting our king and they were hanged, the rulers objected for the hanging, the Anakin Giants picked them up and said: don't you have respect for the King of the earth? And began to squeeze them in their hands and blood came out from their mouth, there body went limp in the hands of the Giants

The godly queens of the devils rushed outside and cried, have mercy o King Judah don't kill us, he took out the rod and began to spank them for making their gods there kings and told them to leave the nation and never return.

Judah pursued with this strategy in surprise attack and conquered the nations of the godly kings to be the king of the earth and after death to be king of the godly spirits. Judah made the godly kings cease by force to be the mighty God of the earth. And made his Israelites Kings in the nations he captured.

The battalion of gods and mankind and Giants went inside the houses and raped the women to populate Mankind, gods, and Giants for the nation and took what was valuable

The gods they captured were made slaves to build the nations for Israelite Kings and the trouble makers to Babylon for burnt offerings in full moons to the unknown god in Hades.

CURSED IS HE THAT LIETH WITH HIS DAUGHTER (DEUT 27.22-26: EPH2.1-22: RO8.9)

Judah returned to the palace in Babylon after fighting all his battles to eliminate the godly kings of the devils to take over there nations to give his Israelites to be Kings of their nations and be the mighty God of the earth.

Judah saw his servants wearing the dresses of Tamuze, he asked why are you dressed in my queens clothes? They answered she gave it to us as a gift, in anger he said where is She? They said she is in the harem with her Mother, Judah said so they are making a fool of God of Israelites and Mankind in the harem.

Judah said to the servants, if I go in the harem, I'll kill her; fetch me a drink, then said if I touch her and she shed one tear Elijah will come after me; this was more he could bear after fighting the godly kings for their nations and threatened by Elijah if he touch Eve or Tamuze Is Hades.

THE QUEEN AND MOTHER DRESSED IN SACK CLOTH (PS30.11:IS 49.23: JER31.33-38)

Judah went in the harem, EVE and Tamuze looked at him, they politely asked him; what you want? Judah had an apple in his hand he said I brought this apple for you Eve, take it, I want your advice. Could you come and talk to me in the Palace?

Eve followed him to the palace when they got inside, Judah locked Eve in a cell in total darkness, and went back to the harem and asked Tamuze and Haddassah who he liked more than his other daughters to come and join him and Eve in the palace. When they got inside Tamuze asked where is my Mother? Judah said come follow me I'll show you, and he locked them in the cell with Eve. And said you will not come out until you worship the God of the whole earth as your King.

Judah went backto the harem and threatened his pregnant daughters for him and said: If any of you give birth to males I will sacrifice them as burnt offering for god and the devils in Hades, the pregnant women pleaded O King have mercy on mankind children from your seed.

A few days went by, he heard no sound in the cell and thought the women would be hungry and submit to worship him as the King of the earth, little did he know the women enjoyed the peace they fell asleep. Judah became curious and went to the cell, he unlocked the door and had a peep inside, and saw Eve and Tamuze were full of light, asleep lighting up the cell.

Judah ran out of the cell thinking it's the Spirits CHRIST and Elijah waiting for him to send him to Hades to the devils to punish him for taking over the throne and Queen Tamuze, terrified, he ran outside and left the cell door opened. After he had a drink to calm his nerves he called the guards to check the cell. They returned and said: The women in the cell wanted water to drink and bread to eat.

Judah was confused he scratched his head said: give them what they asked and tell Eve I want to speak with her, Tamuze could not be bothered and stayed in the cell with Hadassah; Eve followed the guards to meet Judah.

Judah said: Eve I would like you to communicate with Elijah for me. Eve looked at him and said my dead daughter,s children are pregnant to make mankind for you they will be giving birth any time soon and will need assistance giving birth.

There was silence, Eve said: Judah you have brought shame on your mother and me and Elijah who brought you up, and want me to communicate to Elijah for you, I am ashamed and sorry for you. You locked your mother in a cell, you did the same as the devils when you were in her womb, when the devils kidnapped her and held her in captivity in a cell in the palace of devils. You betroth your mother and held her in captivity under the law of devils and made her queen in Babylon.

My daughter has withheld tears so you can humble yourself and ask Elijah to have mercy on you for all the wickedness you have done against my people, Elijah has no pleasure in your wickedness and your hate for holy people, we are the only two holy people left on earth,you should repent and ask for mercy for Elijah to grant you everlasting Peace.

EXHORTATION FROM EVE TO JUDAH

Eve said: Judah, Elijah gave you a choice to have faith for peace but you chose to take the oath of devils to be against Elijah and Christ and exert every sort of evil against them to be a prophet of the law under oath. Elijah gave you a promise before you took the oath that he will abandon you if you went with your mother,He has restrained himself from punishing you with extreme patience.

While you are a king you should use your authority to do good for all you procreated from the seed of god you father (Cain) you passed on his seed to make gods, so before they die and become godly spirits they have a choice to have everlasting Peace and not fall in Hades like god your father for rape.You had a choice to have Faith in Elijah to save yourself, and teach gods and their children so they don't suffer like god your father in Hades for ignorance.

Every god from your seed that pass on the accursed seed procreate like you will hate there mother for giving birth to them to suffer the same way you hate your mother for being born not perfect and need salvation. if they are willing to have faith for their body to be for creation of a new Spirit. Elijah taught you the doctrine of Salvation before you took the doctrine of devils with many faults that lead to Death.

Judah: Eve said, the devils are no more on earth and left you with their law to control the spirits from there seed to fall to them and Death. The devils did not destroy the kingdoms of the flesh of your mother. Before you became King, Elijah prophesy you would be a king of nations, it was for you to do good, and not do like devils. Elijah promised if you went against him you would receive all spirits from your seed in the gate if they have no Faith like you he would remove gods in his sight. Your mother's flesh is her inheritance on earth forever.

Judah said; Eve I hate to give up my spirit for everlasting peace. If Elijah had created a Sprit in my body it would be his Son enjoying life with him forever and not me. It is not righteous I should be asleep while his Son created in my body would be enjoying life with him forever.

THE COVENANT OF PEACE

Eve said you are either a Spirit of creation in the light for the Eternal to accept you to live among angels above, you are of the from the seed of god of the devil who raped me to make god your father and he did the same and raped you mother to make a god like him through no fault of me or your mother we are innocent. This is why you had a choice for salvation for peace because it is not righteous to suffer because of rape.

The devils violated the covenant an statutes of the ETERNAL while they lived among angels in heaven not to make a god with the ETERNAL, s creation, Satan came to earth and raped me to make a god (Cain) your father, this opened the way for Salvation for Elijah to be created in righteousness by the WORD for righteous Judgment on the devils and all godly spirits that has no faith in him to return to the devils and Death for ever.

Eve went on to say, Judah there is no purgatory for godly spirits, neither can a godly spirit be born again, once the spirit of gods separate from the dead body is to face Judgment for everlasting peace or end with devils and Death in the everlasting fire. Elijah gave you the choice to have faith in him to save you from joining god your father in Hades for rape.

CHRIST has faith in Elijah to establish kingdoms from the flesh of your mother to Create new Spirits to continue in the images to be as it was in the beginning by the WORD. Eve said; Judah can you fight against Elijah with the WORD? Judah bowed his head.

THE PROBLEM WITH LIFE ON EARTH

Eve said: Judah do you understand the problem you have caused for mankind and Israelites for hanging the body Adam and slaying all my Sons to be a king with devils? For shedding holy blood on earth you have condemned yourself, and sprits from your seed will face judgment for trespassing in holy flesh of your mother for salvation.

Judah Elijah taught you scripture. What association can your mother's Spirit have with your godly spirit after her body is dead. what have you in common with your mother spirit, you betroth her in the flesh, not in the Spirit, all spirits from your seed is born in her flesh is a god like you and god your father of the devils.

What harmony had the Spirit CHRIST in Adam had with you before you hanged his body on the tree? Did not CHRIST speak to you through the mouth of Adam to go and tell the devils to come and do the hanging? Is it not your envy to be a king with the kings you hanged the body of Adam on a tree. You wanted to be a king with kings through wickedness to have authority over gods to declare war against Elijah for the Earth with godly spirits. Your mother is my daughter from my flesh from her Father's Spirit whose flesh you you were born from the seed of god. You hanged the body of her Father on a Tree.

Through this you have condemned yourself and all godly spirits who has no faith like you will face judgment. Elijah promised you would inherit all spirits from your seed, if any god have no faith in him for salvation, did he make this promise to you yes or no? Judah bowed his head and put his fingers in his ears. He could not bear what Eve was telling him what Elijah had promised him if he fornicate with his mother ill abandon you. Judah you forced your mother to make children to be born to Death.

TRUTH OF EVE

Eve said Judah I am telling you the way it is, what the devil did to me and your mother was a violation and forbidden at all times to make a god with the Eternal creation, it is a immortal sin to make a god to suffer with Death. Every god born is born to trouble, you have locked us up in a cell and an not set us free.

When spirits end in the gate in captivity in everlasting fire tell them is because you did the same as devils and held me and your mother in captivity when you were the king of Babylon, if you continue with your doctrine to hold us in captivity until we dead, multitudes will end in fire with the devils and Death and they will pluck out your eyes for not telling them of the choice to have faith for peace

Eve said; Judah I am telling you so, to warn you of the consequence facing you if you populate the earth to make spirits to fight Elijah with the WORD. You have shed enough blood on earth, if its your desire to shed more blood, I am sorry for you and the godly spirits who will fight with you for the earth.

Eve said I have made myself very clear to you to warn you if that is your plan so you cannot say I did not warn you. If god your father had faith you would not be born he chose to follow devils and you made the same mistake like him and boasting it is your wickedness that made you a king it is his wickedness that made him end in Hades for rape to end with Death. Eve said I am telling you all this so you don't blame me for not telling you the truth before another god is born and don't have faith like you.

Instead of giving Elijah praise for adopting you and taught you skill and to obey, you have become a disobediant foolish king like the devils. (Mt 5.1-12: Deut32.15.21) who left the good life to be among creatures on earth.

TAMUZE AND HADASSAH (NAH 3.4:MIC7.6)

After Eve spoke to Judah, Tamuze and Hadassah came from the cell said to Hadassah: Behold your mighty God, and said to Judah, did the devils have peace on earth for fucking me to make gods to populate the earth? How can I have peace, you are evil and wanted to strangle me. I will stay with my Mother and my dead sister's children who are pregnant for you to assist with the birth of your mankind children in the harem for peace.

Judah got angry with hate and annoyed and said: all of you get the hell out of my sight before I shed blood in the palace, as they began to walk away, Judah asked Hadassah to stop. She was young and beautiful and could not have enough of him in the harem. She said what you want with me? Judah said: If you kneel down and worship your king, you can stay in the palace.

Hadassah said: O king, I worship you to Death make me your mistress, and she stayed in the palace.

BABYLON THE MOTHER OF PROSTITUTES (17.5-6)

A MAN HAS TWO WIVES ONE HATED ONE LOVED (DEUT 21.15)

Tamuze took a good look at them and said good bye teach Hadassah scripture so she don't fall and cry, Judah said I am who I am, no faith no peace I can't be born again.

Eve said come my blessed daughter, you have found Elijah your savior who you can trust to protect you from Judah from now on for peace, and went hand in hand back to the harem dressed in sack clothes to be among the pregnant women for Judah.

JUDAH AND HADASSAH BLACK AND BEAUTIFUL (NAH3.4; CAN1.5:PS45.1.15)

Judah took Hadassah on his chariot and went to the city, she got fitted with embroidered clothes, her gown interwoven with gold, and everything she wanted precious stones and gold armbands, fragrant oils, perfume to smell nice for Judah

For the first ten months Judah took Hadassah everywhere and introduced her to the military, officials in government, and merchants in Babylon she was elegantly dressed with precious stones and armband in gold.

Hadassah went with Judah to new moon burnt offerings of gods to god in Hades they went to the Olympian to see Giants fighting each other to Death. This brought much excitement to Judah and Hadassah to see Giants fighting each other to death.

Judah and Hadassah were compatible in everything in with wickedness, she became famous in Babylon. Hadassah encouraged Judah to bring her sisters from the Harem to live in the palace.

She invited rulers, merchants, Israelites to the palace and they would go in the room with the statue of god in Hades to defile the women in front of the statue to make mankind with her sisters. Hadassah and her sisters did what the men wanted, if they complained Judah would get angry and beat them up.

The sisters of Hadassah got pregnant in the palace, when they gave they gave birth to babies that did not look like Israelites, Judah would cast in the furnace in the palace as a burnt offering. And would say you should not make gods for burnt offering.

Hadassah said, My king your excessive lust for whores will be discovered one day for making my sisters whore for you. Judah got angry and said, you are a whore, your mother was raped by devils and you are my whore and you will do the same as your mother, you are corrupt like me if you don't do as I say I will pluck out your breast.

My excessive lust with you is little compared with the giants who fucked your mother's mother with big ones like horses. Hadassah said: you commit incest with me and warned me if I bear gods you will cast them in fire as a burnt offering to god in Hades who fucked you mother, don't you like to look like a god my father?.

Judah said Hadassah you are my favourite daughter, I chose to make mankind to be my creation, you are my olive branch, The Giants you went with in the palace are your brothers, their mothers and your mother are sisters I brought up in the harem from birth.

You and I are born in sin and corrupt with excessive lust there is no cure for us born in filth of our fathers, but when we are spirits I will see the god who passed on the accursed to me to make you a whore and you will see the devil who raped you mother,s mother to make us no acceptable above.

Judah went on to say, Hadassah I took you from the harem to the palace, made you a elegant whore wearing nice clothes with jewelry, you paint your eye lids when you go in the city to shop, when you come to bed you want me to fuck you like a whore with incense in the room, no one can purge this lewdness out of you but I with all my wickedness till you are dead in Babylon.

FEAR OF ELIJAH

Judah began to stay in the palace more and more and became passive and submissive to the sexual appetite of Hadassah excessive desire to have sex they feasted, got drunk and rejoiced in their passion for each other, anything Hadassah wanted Judah gave her and became his mistress and running of the palace.

The people in the nations saw less and less of tyrant who called himself the mighty God living a solitary life in the palace and saw more and more of Hadassah in Babylon while queen Tamuze was not seen at all by the gods who worshiped her as the mother of gods. Hadassah became popular with the merchants they would give her any Jewelry she liked for a favour with Judah. She got apartments in the city and took her sisters from the palace and made them Whore, and used their apartments to entertain her lovers

She began to involve herself in witchcraft to cast a spell on Judah to be the queen of Babylon, She was beautiful and every male wanted to have sex with her, her beauty went to her head she took the same cup Judah made her drink his piss and did the same to him, this made Judah mad in the Palace.

Judah held her by her throat and began to strangle her. She urged a spirit of the dead to loosen his grip she spat in his face and he fell on the floor shaking.

Hadassah ran to the harem to Eve, The children from her sisters were glad to see her, when they came up to her to she shouted at them, don't touch my clothes you are not clean, go away.

Tamuze said: The favourite mistress who selleth her sisters for whoredom is back in the harem.

DAUGHTER INLAW AGAINST MOTHER INLAW

Tamuze said: Hadassah, you were born in this harem, Judah took your children with him to mix with mine to make Israelites now you re his mistress and don't want his children with your sister to touch your clothes.

Hadassah got angry and said who the fuck you are to talk to me? I am his daughter and deserve to live in the palace. I made mankind for him in the harem while you lived in the palace, he took the best of my children to procreate with yours to make Israelites and she slaped Tamuze on her face. Tamuze fled from the harem for peace.

Eve said:Hadassah you slapped my blessed daughter among the women in this harem you should not do that, she left the palace to be a hand maid to your sister,s children you have become cruel like your father who made you here to be his mistress and sell your children, who were not good looking, My shame is against your father.

Hadassah pushed Eve and hurried outside and asked the horseman to take her to the city. She had many lovers among them were Giants. They excited her.

Judah became unattractive with long beard sulking and complaining about her absence from the palace and was afraid to be alone. Judah could not satisfy the excessive passion Hadassah had for sex he became possessive. He heard the horseman pulled up outside the palace.

As she got inside, Judah said my mistress it is late. Hadassah looked at him then said; what is it? I did to you the same you did to my mother with the cup with my libation to drink as an offering to god in Hades and you began chocking me, I am not anymore like the little maid you brought up in the harem who was stupid with your plan to make mankind for you to procreate.

You are God my father, I did everything you wanted in the harem to please you and made many children for you to mix with children with your Queen to make Israelites, your queen chose to live in the harem to be a hand maid, I am your daughter, mistress you made to be your whore in your palace with many men in your bed. Your queen is over the wall, why don't you ask her to come back and stay in the palace with you and I will stay with my sisters in the city? Eve said her shame is against you, when you fall she will rise and Elijah will judge between Tamuze and me and when I fall in the ruble of Babylon Tamuze will rise. Who is this Elijah? Judah said; Hadassah don't pay any attention to what Eve said she is jealous of you and I in the palace. Hadassah said, if the tower of Babel falls and cover me in ruble, mankind and Israelites will know you are not honest with me.

Judah began to tremble in fear of being alone, said Hadassah don't leave me I am in fear for my life, I will give you anything you want, he needed her more than she needed him, she had lovers in Babylon and wanted power to rule as the queen of Babylon.

Hadassah said; my king, you said you will give me anything I want; I want us to have a banquet in the palace to celebrate the Passover to be queen in the palace. All the holy people are dead, Eve and your queen are the only holy ones left on earth let them be the sacrifice for the Passover so I can be queen of Babylon.

Judah said it is an excellent idea to celebrate this Passover for all mankind to worship my beautiful queen as their mother and for Israelites and mankind to worship us as King and queen who created them and to fight with us when we are godly spirits to celebrate the victory for the earth.

Hadassah said before Eve and Tamuze perish let us celebrate. Hadassah invited the Israelite kings, merchants, astrologers, magicians and her lovers in the military who wanted her to be queen of Babylon

TAMUZE QUEEN OF BABYLON

Tamuze fled from the harem after Hadassah slapped her and went in the wilderness, she stopped to have a rest to meditate. Elijah appeared to her and asked; Where are you going? She said O Elijah I am fed up living this stressful life it is more than I can bear, I left the palace from this tyrant for peace and his mistress she came to the harem and slapped me in the face in front of the children because I told her she should be more kind to them.

Elijah said: Tamah you must return, suffer your shame and have faith in me, How else can you ask gods and Israelites to have mercy on you for making them through no fault of yours to receive forgiveness. The shame of Judah will multiply Kingdoms from your flesh exceedingly to create Spirits in kingdoms worthy for Salvation for your shame and affliction.

ELIJAH PROMISS TAMAH A SON BY THE WORD

Elijah said I will give you a Son by the WORD, it is not a hard thing for me and through him the earth will have Sprits populating the earth in Kingdoms from your flesh in multitudes, this is my Promise to you, so be patient your time for peace will come. Elijah vanished and she returned to be with Eve and told her mother Elijah promise to give her a Son by the WORD to populate righteous children in her flesh.

THE BANQUET TO CELEBRATE WITH KING JUDAH AND HIS MISTRESS HADASSAH

Judah made his Israelites kings in the nations he conquered and they were among the guest in the palace in BABYLON.Hadassah made herself beautiful dressed in purple and scarlet material gold armbands with coloured stones, eye shadow and make up, everyone complimented her for her beauty, the guests congratulated Judah for his new mistress.

After everyone had eaten and drank and congratulated Judah for his victory in the Nations and making his Israelites Kings to rule the nations of the gods of the devils. King Judah stood to give a speech and there was silence.

He stretched out his hands and said, behold and pointed his hand at each of his Israelites kings and princes, then pointed his hand at the rulers of mankind and his commandant of gods and there was silence. He looked at all of them without a word. Then he pointed his finger in the direction where Eve and Tarmuze was in the harem, then pointed his hand above.

Then he began to boast, I have multiplied from the flesh Tamuze and my mistress, all of you are my creation, and not like what the devils made with my queen. By my strength and wisdom I removed the devils from the earth and taken the Hebrew women they raped to make gods and Giants, from their children I created all of you to be my people on earth. Everyone began to clap and said we worship you created us all, you are a mighty God.

Then there was silence, he said I removed the godly Kings of the devils from the nations and made my Israelites Kings in their nation to rule mankind and gods and Giants on earth with my wisdom.

When I found the Hebrew women bound by devils, I gathered them like eggs from hens. No god opened there mouth to save the women. I brought them in my harem and yoked my seed and made you kings and princes and mankind in fertile eggs so you can multiply in abundance on earth to live under the law with my authority.

A Giant stood up and said let us give praise to the king of all nations. A Israelite stood up and said. We worship you father and love our mother while we live in her flesh you are our mighty God. Mankind said, cheers we will make mankind to populate one end of the earth to the other faster than Israelites for you.

King Judah went on to say, My sin to make Israelites and Mankind will stretch the flesh of the queen of Babylon and my mistress with sprits to make multitudes of different images all over the earth to have Spirits with knowledge an wisdom to ascend to the heavens like the brute in my father,s image. If any of his visitors from heaven come to earth they will be punished.

Her Giant lover stood up and said, god in Hades save the king. Hadassah gave Judah a kiss.

THE ISRAELITE KINGS OF JUDAH
(11KI 14.28: 8.23)

The elder king stood up and said we give you praise father for creating us and made us kings to rule nations with your law he held up his cup with wine and said: behold the mighty God the King of Kings of the earth with knowledge of hidden secrets of the Spirit in the image.

Our God has made us his Israelites to do battle with him against this Spirit for the earth, so we can be one flock populating the earth from his seed. The kings and princes said, cheers, mankind said, woe if we lose this battle against this secret Spirit.

Another King said: behold Mighty God and king who conquered the nations of godly kings of the devils to change the course of history for Israelites to rule all nations on earth forever. Let us rejoice with our Mighty God the king of kings achievement for creating multitudes mixing different images in different shades as his creation which the devils could not do, he stopped and looked at every one and there was silence

Another king said: The battle to fight the godly kings of the devils in there nations was a prototype of this real battle to come in the future to fight this unknown Spirit in the light in the image that is coming to fight for the earth.

Hadassah seating next to Judah said: I praise thee, you comfort me with joy, we will be together in this battle as King and queen of the spirits my king. Judah said Hadassah from now on you are my star and queen of Babylon, Tamuze is a burden to me and will not return to the palace.

Hadassah said O king make me your queen, we have the same desire and passion to be king and queen of the whole earth and she went on her knee and began to lick the dust from under his feet and said this is how I want the Passover to be with no holy people on earth.

GIANTS

Judah realized he is not accepted above and propagate Giants to fight his spiritual war for the earth. Elijah made him wise in scripture and he thought he was wiser than Elijah and challenged Elijah for the earth

Elijah took his challenge seriously and gave Judah a lot of years to set up his plan for war up to the time of Salvation for Judgment to return all spirits of gods that has no faith in him in the gate to judah and the devils as he promised, The giant babies he called Anakins and made them his warriors and to protect Israelites. The Neplm Giants, Captorin Giants, zuzansim Giants, were of the Anak Giants mixed with mankind and gods they took the names of the Giant devils and began to populate on earth with different features.

Hadassah had a dream and said; My God, I had a dream. Judah said what was it my queen, Hadassah said I saw two Spirits and they were dazzling me in the Light, then one went in the body of Tamuze an cast out the spirit from the body she was in, and the spirit looked like you and you went in the body of a Israelite.

Then I looked and saw the other Sprit that dazzled me went inside the body of my grandmother Eve he cast out the sprit that look like you my God that was in the same body with her Spirit was in, and the godly spirit look like the statue of the unknown god in the dungeon my sister and I did whoring for you in the palace and the spirit went in the body of an Israelite.

The Spirit came out from my grandmother and it looked like mankind and began speaking telling mankind to repent, they asked him where he came from he said he is a witness with the WORD for all who was slain by one who was crying in the wilderness from birth.

Then I looked and saw the other Spirit that went inside the body of Tamuze was in and became a Hebrew and began to walk among mankind and Israelites when the godly spirits saw him they began to cry we just returned from the heat and they ran in the lake, they were in fear to return in fire

Judah said Hadassah I repent for making mankind with you to mix and mingle to make Israelites with Tamuze to give them grief, after they are dead, they will be as wicked like us and do like the devils to live to Death

Hadassah you are beautiful and you will be my queen to rule the earth when we are spirits to seduce spirits in the flesh to pass on my seed to populate the earth with disease to be spirits like us to prevent salvation. Adam warned me CHRIST will come after me If I Committed abomination while I am in the flesh of his daughter

Judah said Hadassah the statue in the dungeon where you and your sisters whore in front of the unknown god, in truth he is my father in Hades he is my mothers, brother by her mother but not of the same father, swear to me you will not deal falsely with me with our god Belhadassah.

Hadassah said O my God I am like an olive in your hand from youth, you chastised me to do everything that pleaseth thee, you are a god that has pleasure in wickedness. Judah said you were the one I loved the most of all your sisters in the harem I said to myself I will make mankind with you to make all kinds of people beautiful like you on earth. The dream you had they all must have faith in the secret Spirit to rest in peace or join us in the gate.

Hadassah said my God how can we have everlasting life? We are gods from the seed of the god in Hades you say is your father, we are not blessed and born in sin I made mankind for you what is going to happen to them?

Judah replied only there body of all mankind is blessed, their spirits are like ours. The promise is for the kingdoms from our children for Salvation for their spirits to rest in peace.

Hadassah said you commit incest with me and abomination with Tamuze, when she die she will go above and inherit the bodies of mankind and I will inherit the spirits that that has no faith in the gate with you, we did all the hard work with excessive sex to make mankind in our sin to live by the law for their body to be created with Sprits to go above

Judah said its not our fault if our spirit have excessive sex while we live in the flesh which is holy righteous, this fault is with the devils who passed on the seed to god my father who passed it on to me and all mankind is passing on the accursed seed to one another for Death

Hadassah said what about the Israelites with Tamuze. You committed much incest to mix with hers to look like Hebrews you killed. Much blood was spilled on earth from my grandmother Sons; will they have preference over mankind?

Judah said no my daughter, they are from my seed with this curse only there kingdoms that is righteous same as mankind for salvation. Hadassah said, so my God all this fucking to populate the earth in sin is for the secret Spirit in the image of god your father, to pick and choose kingdoms from our sweat, it is not fare this salvation. Judah said in the time of salvation every spirit will have a choice to choose to have faith for everlastingl peace or join us in the gate, if they do the same as you in excess to kill, 763+cheat, be jealous make war with hate against holy people like us. Unless they have a desire to celibate to stop passing the accursed seed and give up sex, they will be like me who had a Choice for eternal peace and chose to be wicked an blasphemous to be a king with authority to be the ruler of the earth for Death. At least they have a Choice for everlasting peace so they don't come crying to me in the gate.

THE FEAR OF DEATH HIDDEN FOR AGES
(COL 1.24-26)

Hadassah said: This is what the mystery Spirit revealed to me in a vision, I saw the spirit Death in flames of fire which the devils did not want you to know, and kept it a secret from you when you took the oath, if you disobey with their law and fail to rule the earth, all spirits from the accursed seed will be punished by Death in the fire. Why do you want mankind and Israelites to worship you to Death? You make all on earth call you a Mighty God who removed the devils from the earth.

Judah said it is this fear of Death and devils that make me wicked for all on earth to worship me and put there hope in me after they are dead for their spirit to fight with me for the earth, as I don't know where devils are since they left the earth.

Elijah will not accept us because we are not perfect like the Hebrews, we are children of rape born in sin, neither can we be born again or change our spirit to be like Spirit of Hebrews to be accepted above to live among angels.

Hadassah said my God so this law of devils is for spirits to worship you for Death? Judah said my mother never worship me, she call me a rebel, a Maduk, a serpent, I choose you to be the mother of mankind to populate the earth like the dust you licked from under my feet.

Hadassah said my God we are counted as nothing and not worthy of salvation, the spirits from your seed are like us counted as nothing, fucking making kingdoms for salvation, the more they fuck is the more kingdoms they will make for Elijah and the Spirit that dazzled me, they will only take the best kingdoms for creation. This makes me angry to be wicked be like you.

You knew all this before you took the Law under oath of the devils; You had me to make mankind for you to live to Death. When they are godly spirits they will know the truth and want to pluck out my eyes for making them not perfect like Hebrews and call me a whore that made them with a God that cannot save them from devils and Death in the fire we should make the two Hebrews left, Tamuze and Eve suffer for the Passover to remove the Hebrews from the earth for Israelites and mankind to populate the earth with godly spirits in abundance.

Judah said it is true the two Hebrews left are among us, but we are spirits in their flesh, if we kill them there blood be on our hands and all spirits of mankind will be condemned and curse us for making them to suffer Death.

CONDEMNATION, TRIAL, TEMPTATION (JA 1.2-18)

Hadassah said my King the two Hebrews left ought to suffer, because we were born in sin to suffer after we are dead like god your father in Hades for rape and passing the accursed seed to you to make me your mistress and whore.

Let this Passover be celebrated with a feast to be remembered in all generation on earth so they may know mother and daughter Passover the earth to mankind and Israelites to sin to Death. After they are dead my king it will be the end of Hebrews on earth, there will be no Hebrews left to tell Israelites and mankind it is through incest we made them and I was your whore, the Truth will be hidden.

MANKIND DO NOT BE DECIEVED (JA.1.19-27)

Hadassah said: my king as long as mankind are on the earth there will be no Hebrew to testify Mankind and Israelites were born in sin like us and must have faith and have a choice to have eternal peace.

ELIJAH WILL SAVE HIS PEOPLE (HOS 13.3-17:JA1.2-8)

Judah said: Hadassah, Elijah said to me if Tamuze or Eve shed one tear he will come after me. I am afraid if I did any wickedness to them I will leave the earth in a whirl wind I am afraid what the devils will do to me.mankind and Isrelites will be fatherless and live to Death Satan will tear me apart for taking over his throne to make Israelites and the other devils will kick my ass for making mankind with your mother. While they are in the heat, I will be alone fighting devils. Now I fear for my life, god my father will laugh at me for not having faith like him to have peace. Hadassah said: O my God when you die hide yourself so Elijah don't send you to the devils let us put this faith to the test to see if Elijah will save us we have commited much sin, if he don't save us he will not save mankind and Israelites spirits from Death.

JUDAH CRIES IN HIS SLEEP

Judah began crying in his sleep and it woke up Hadassah, She said O my King why are you Crying? Judah said I had a dream and saw Adam I hanged and saw a Spirit coming out of his body and it was going up to heaven, then he came after me for was casting out the Spirits from the flesh of Eve and Tamuze and I was running and in fear of him catching me.

Then I saw Children all over the earth in the light in multitudes coming out from the bodies of mankind and Israelites, and the spirits cast out was falling on top of each other and pointing their fingers at me saying it is your fault for hanging the body Adam on the tree and saw them going to the deep.

Hadassah said what can this mean? You were screaming in your sleep scaring me, he said I saw Elijah in the dream with Tamuze and

Eve and He began speaking WORDS and saw their Spirit leaving there Body in fire and going above and the Spirit in the Light that left the boby of Adam saying to Elijah Vengence is mine for killing all my Sons and holding Eve and Tamuze in Captivity, Hadassah I am scared.

Hadassah said you are scaring me with this dreams. I can't sleep this Spirit is angry with you, our sin has reached into heaven and want us out of our body to fall to be with the spirits you saw falling to the deep.

Judah said: our incest have brought much trouble to mankind and they will do the same and provoke the Spirit in the Light in Heaven and He will come and take vengeance and cast all spirits until there is none left on earth to stop fornication for Death.

Hadassah said: I will see Belhadassah our first god he interpret dreams, have rest my king, I have to prepare the Passover feast and want it to be remembered from generation to generation.

Hadassah went to see Belhadassah to interpret the dreams, he said the dreams is because you have no mercy on your mother and her mother and hold them in captivity, you been wicked to your queen mother in the palace and the Spirit will come after our father.

Judah said: have I not made you mother of mankind and made you my mistress? By my power I will make you queen of Babylon to rule with majesty.

Hadassah said the Spirit spoke through the mouth of Belhadassah and said when your sprit depart from your body your spirit will be caught in the tempest to be with devils for slapping his daughter, and to tell the devil you raped your mother ad the Spirit CHRIST Rule in

Kingdoms through Elijah with the WORD. And you had knowledge of the ETERNAL and CHRIST before you took the oath of devils to live to Death you had no Faith and blasphemed Christ and Elijah to be a prophet to gods. O my king you are God of god, there is no hope for eternal peace now. 0r be the King of Israelites forever.

Judah said I had another dream, I saw multitudes of spirits of gods in a tempest falling in the deep water and they were swimming to a trap door and I saw fire in the water and it began bubble like hot water. Then I saw multitudes of children pointing their hands at me saying murderer, murderer and was going up to heaven to see judgment on me.

Hadassah said: These dreams you are having is frightening me, these spirits that went to see judgment on thee hate you for spilling holy blood, these Spirits has no fear of you, you are a mighty God don't let these dreams frighten you, Ill see Belhadassah to interpret your dreams.

Hadassah saw Belhadassah and he said: Tell our father the great Spirit will come to remove him from the earth for his wickedness. She said my King, Belhadassah said, he hope all women from mankind think twice before they fuck to bring another god to add to your sin, and he began to cry and said, Hadassah I regret I made mankind to be sinners. Death told the king of devils he wants every spirits from his seed to return to him in the fire if they fail to conquer the worlds. Hadassah said: You are a God of god who created mankind, you are a mighty King with the ancient devils use your power to scare this Elijah and CHRIST to stop these dreams. (Dan47.2)

Judah said: Hadassah all mankind is passing on my seed to populate our wickedness to one another, it is late to stop incest for brothers and sisters to be born in sin to live to Death. They will be corrupting flesh with the disease of Death. Hadassah said: tell Elijah to have mercy on us and we will let his people go. Judah said: It is Elijah with the WORD I am afraid of what he will do to me, he has a plan for Salvation. My time for salvation is past since I took the oath of devils,Hadassah said; Belhadassah said, the kingdom is departing from you, your time is coming to an end as king on earth and your spirit will be in a tempest taken to a place where there is no flesh or water to drink, O my king there is no salvation for thee when you die save me from Elijah.

THE QUEENS OF THE ISRAELITES KINGS HAVE A VISION OF THE END (REV9.15-19)

One of the queens said to her Isralite king: O my king, I had a dream of the Passover.her king said what is it my love? She said: I saw a woman taken by the tempest and she fell in a furnace and she was crying for God our father to save her.

Then I saw in a dream 200000 million spirits released from the furnace and they began to swim till they came above the sea and they went all over the earth and began to enter mankind to seduce them to kill mankind to be godly spirits and they began to do battle with God our father for the earth.

Then I saw the spirits that were released and went into the body of mankind came against the Spirit in the Light, he spoke the WORD and the spirits in the tempest began falling into fire, I was afraid and He said to me it is because these spirits had no faith him

Then I saw the Spirits fast asleep, then they awake and was in the Light coming out of the earth and they began waving at me saying to me have faith for peace. What do you think my king of these dreams? The Israelite King said the Spirits in the light was from the body of those that had faith and wanted peace.

Another queen said to her king: O my king I had a dream. The king said, what did you dream this time? She said I saw flames in the earth with sprits crying saying, O God save us the devils are angry with us saying God our father is sending spirits that don't look like gods to them while he is enjoying himself above the earth with queen Tamuze they were crying and telling me to tell their brothers and sisters to have faith so they don't come in the fire to face angry devils.

Another queen said to her Israelite king, O my king I had a dream, he said what is it my love? We are going to be late for the Passover feast. She said it will take a minute, I saw spirits falling from the sky in the mouth of the waters, and a Spirit in the Light came up to me and said they are spirits of your God father who refuse to have faith for peace they fell to be with devils. then I saw spirits fast asleep and were no more seen, then I saw the earth with multitudes of spirits in the light and they began waving their hands at me what do you think is the meaning of this dream? The king said they want you to tell our children to tell their children to have faith to sleep for ever.

Another queen said to her king: O my king I had a dream this one frightened me. He said, we are going to be late, you know father will be angry if we are late for the feast, She said this Spirit in the light said no spirit from our father is accepted above if they have no faith like our father they will fall in the furnace. I began to run in my dream to save our children but God our father appeared and said to the spirit in the Light we are his inheritance and wanted them for war

Another queen said to her king; I had a dream of our mother and her Hebrew mother they were standing in front of multitudes on earth and they ask God our father to repent for making gods to be sinners on earth, our father and multitudes of spirits began to cry we just came from Hades have mercy.

The great Sprit in the Light appeared and the spirits began to run away in fear before he spoke a word to send them back to Hades, I saw fire in the deep and our father and the spirits vanished, then I looked up and saw our grandmother sitting next to the great Spirit in the Light on a throne.

Then I heard a voice saying do not delay, the mystery of the SPIRIT in the Light is known to thee, go to the feast and tell the liar to tell mankind the truth before they make war with him for the earth

Another queen said: my king I had a terrible dream and it made me cry. This one was worse than the last one, I saw Two Spirits in the Light, One went in the body of our mother and the other Spirit went in the body of our Grandmother

Then suddenly a spirit that looked like our father was cast out of the same body our Mother was in and went in the body of our brother, the other Spirit that went in the body of our Grandmother cast out a spirit that looked like the unknown god and the spirit went the body of one of our brothers and he began to cry

Then the two Sprits in the Light that went in the body of our mother and grandmother became human and began walking and talking among mankind and Israelites one of the Spirit went one way and began to say, godly spirits in the body of mankind all of you are sons of murderers and prostitutes come and repent.

The other Spirit was walking among mankind telling them things about God our father and Hadassah and was commanding godly spirits to come out of the body of our brothers and they threw our brothers on the ground crying don't send us back in the heat have mercy.

One of the Spirit said to our father he could not have our mother you are from Death, our father got angry and cut off his head and I began to cry. My king I don't feel good go to the Passover feast.The king said if we don't go to support father he will be angry with us we have to go.

THE TEN ISRAELITE KINGS (PS5.2:DAN2.47)

The kings met before the feast of the Passover and they began to discussing the dreams there queens had, they all had sex with Hadassah and kept it as there secrete from each other in fear what God would do to them if he knew.

Hadassah sat next to God, dressed in Scarlet and gold with emerald stones around her neck, she held a gold cup with blood, she was happy seeing all her lovers under the same roof to celebrate the Passover feast.

The commander of the battalion of soldiers who witnessed the hanging of the body (CHRIST) Adam and slaying of all his Sons stood to give a speech, said: King Judah, we give thee praise to you God almighty you made mankind with beautiful Hadassah and made Israelites with our mother and also made gods we worship you to Death

A Israelite King stood up and said: Hail king of kings and God of god, your greatness has gone from the earth to the heavens, we worship you forever and give you praise for creating us.

Hadassah whispered my King I wish Belhadassah was here to the feast,he said; Belhadassah will be back my love, Hadassah had contempt for the Israelites kings and determined to make Belhadassah her king, Judah had taken Balhadassah away from her and gave him to a god to adopt, he was wise among the gods and became popular predicting the future for gods did sorcery and interpreted dreams. Hadassah found out where Belhadassah was and became involved with witchcraft to have power to rule.

All the guests arrived to celebrate the Passover of the kingdom to King Judah, there was music, eating and drinking wine: King Judah whispered in the ear of Hadassah what is your petition it be given thee; Hadassah said I am fed up of being your mistress If I am beautiful in your eyes make me queen of Babylon.

Judah said worship your mighty God to Death. Hadassah knelt before him took her hair and wiped the dust from under his feet in tears and licked under his feet and said, this is how you have to complete the Passover for the earth with your me to rule with your creation with no Hebrews, Judah took the crown and put it on her head and sat next to him.

A Israelite king stood up and said let us give praise to our God and his queen for all on earth to worship them to Death.

The ten Israelite kings came and prostrate before God and Queen Hadassah for making mankind to be free from the sin of devils and making Israelites his peculiar people to rule all on earth by the law.

After this speech they began to sing by the river of Babylon to King God and Queen Hadassah, when they were through singing, Judah stood up and thanked them for giving him praise and worship and said my Queen is my shining star as long as there is darkness in the world worship her to make beautiful children.

Judah said: Hadassah now they will idolize you and make you there star of the earth, what is your next petition? Hadassah said if I am your star of the earth you should have one queen on earth. You are a God in wickedness and hate, I am a jealous queen and don't want to share your throne with your Hebrew Queen in the harem.

THE PASSOVER IN BABYLON

Let the last two Hebrews come with my sisters children to worship you my mighty God and your Queen,then sacrifice them to complete the Passover of kingdoms from their flesh to you to wipe the Hebrews from the earth like the dust I licked clean from under your feet, so the memory of holy people perish from the face of the earth as long as there is darkness in the world to prevent the truth of your incest with me is spoken from the mouth any one on earth. (Jer7.28)

Judah whispered in her ear, Hadassah these Hebrews are difficult are they have no fear of Death, if they don't worship what is your next wish? Hadassah said let them be eaten by the hungry lions in the den to hide we were born in sin and made mankind to be sinners populate in our sin.

Hadassah said my King they put their Faith in Elijah, so let us see if Elijah will save them from being the sacrifice for the Passover to rule all on earth with your Queen. Judah said if I send them to the den of lions and they shed one tear Elijah will come and tear out my heart before our guests.

Hadassah said they will not have time to shed a tear the lions will eat them and you will be the conqueror of the earth and we will have it written, God is more powerful than Elijah after the lions eat them. If you don't have the victory in the lions den everyone will say you did not create us in this world, you are a father of liars.(Jn8.44)

Judah began to tremble, Hadassah if the lions eat them there Spirit will come after me, the Spirits I have in my dreams torment me., Hadassah said you are God with authority over all spirits, no spirit of the dead can come after us I will be a bitch if they attack us they will do as I say, we must not be afraid, let the two Hebrews come and worship God of this World and your Queen before our guests as our witness, if they don't worship us cast them in the den of lions as the sacrifice to complete the Sabbath of blood of the holy people to Passover the Kingdom from their flesh to make spirits.

HE THAT COVERETH HIS SINS SHALL NOT PROSPER (PRO 28.13:MT10.26)

Judah called the guard and said: bring Eve and queen Tamuze and the children in the harem to worship your God and Queen Hadassah before our guests.

The guard brought Eve, and Queen Tamuze and the children from the harem they stood before Judah and Hadassah, the guard said don't stand there, kneel down and worship our God and Queen Hadassah.

Eve said to the guard, we will not worship your God or Hadassah who is your Queen. It is they who should worship us they are not blessed or holy pure, it is you who should worship them, we don't worship anyone that is born in sin like you in my flesh through no fault of yours, you should have faith in Elijah to save you from the beast who has put fear in you to worship him as your God with his jealous queen.

Eve went onto say your God want to eliminate us from the earth to celebrate the Passover with his guests we are not afraid, if we die we will live and be in a place where you cannot come. My shame to make a god I will endure and the shame of my daughter to make a god sitting on the throne with his daughter she will endure. My advice to all of you seek peace before it is to late.

The guests was silence, Eve went on to say Your God is a god of god who passed on the accursed seed to you to live to Death, everything about Death should not be hidden and should be known, the truth has been hidden from you for ages, before I perish I speak the truth before all of you in this feast by words from my mouth so you have faith for peace and not fall. For what will be written after the Passover will be words from liars to hide the truth from their lewdness.

The guests began to laugh and looked at Eve and Tamuze standing there in sack cloth amazed. Judah said to Eve, shut up, Eve said I will not shut up you will deceive many if I don't speak the truth and have it written it's a lie. You have eliminating all my Sons and keep the knowledge of salvation to yourself so no one on earth will know the choice for peace, and the way to everlasting life.

Eve told the guests: You have made Judah your mighty God and King he has blinded your eyes and corrupted your minds so you don't have faith for peace so your body can be for creation with a New Spirit with everlasting life. If you are content to be the way you are, worship your God to save you and don't blame me for not telling you the truth.

The guests began to cough Judah was angry, scared of Eve shedding a tear. Eve said to Hadassah from your youth you Idolize your king, he has made you his queen and his Star for making mankind with you, we have one judge who has power to save and destroy, if we shed one tear in this Passover feast you will fall to meet god his father to tell you the truth why his crying.

Hadassah rushed at Eve and gave her a slap on her face, and said how dare you talk to my father this way in front of our guests,are you are jealous? She pushed Eve and she fell on the floor. Then shouted at Tamuze you fucking bitch making Israelites with my children, she pushed Tamuze and she fell, Hadassah put her feet on Tamuze stomach, took a cup with blood and poured it over her to humiliate her in front of her Israelite kings stamping on her stomach. (Ps1.37:Oba 4-17)

The Israelite kings could not help their mother in this confrontation in fear Hadassah would tell Judah she had sex with them in front of the guests and there queens, she looked at Judah and said: now let us celebrate the Passover my God and King, send them to den of lions to feast.

All the guests eyes was on their God, he had a gold cup with blood in his hands and said woe is unto me Hadassah when the lions feast on their flesh, I will have no one else but you my queen in the world.

The guards took Eve and Tamuze and the last of the children of Judah with his daughters to the lion's den, they rolled the stone so the lions could come out, the lions entered looked at the guards and began to roar at them and they ran away.

The lions came to Eve and Tamuze and began to stand on their hind legs and lick the face of Eve and Tamuze the children began to stroke their back then took turns riding the lions, the lions began to run round in circles in the den then lay and fell asleep. (EZ1-6)

The guards returned to the Passover feast and said: O God the lions have eaten the women and children, Judah said in Hadassah ear all Tamuze wanted is peace, Hadassah said now I am your queen to rule with you and not your queen under the law that became the sacrifice for the Passover, they began to celebrate the Passover with their guests.

One of the princes appointed to minister to God and Hadassah said: Let us celebrate the Passover feast and praise to our God for putting an End to the holy people on earth, let us bless our God and his queen Hadassah who has made us participate in shedding the blood of the holy people.

The guests said: We bless our God who sit on his throne with his Queen Hadassah and mindful to live by his law from this generation to all generations. The second prince brought a loaf of bread on a platter to God (Judah) he took the loaf and broke it and took a crumb from it and passed it over to Hadassah she took a crumb and said pass it among the guest and they did the same to the last crumb. Then Judah said we are all from the same loaf passing the accursed seed from god of the devil in Hades.

The next prince brought a platter with meat to God (Judah) sliced a small peace and said to Hadassah take a piece and share it among the guests, then said all of you live in the flesh of the two holy women that was the Passover..

The next prince brought a gold cup full of blood he took a sip and passed it Hadassah she had a sip and said to the prince pass it to the guest to sip as a testament to this Passover so it be celebrated from generation to generation to participate in shedding the blood of holy people on earth. Then belly dancers were dancing to the music and singers were singing there is no god like our God from this world.

Hadassah asked Judah/God: Why did you not let the devils hang the body of my Grand Father to see his reaction, now you killed his wife and daughter you made princes and princess with her who sit with us as kings today while Belhadassah is somewhere in Babylon among gods. You said one day he will come back to me, I suffered much pain in child birth to make your first son for you and he is not here to give you praise for all your hard work in creating Mankind and Israelites.

Judah said, Hadassah I chose you from all my daughters to make beautiful children like you, all women of mankind in this generation is making beautiful children like you and they will be making children with beautiful images all over the earth from generation to generation let us celebrate.

THE WRITING ON THE WALL
(EZ13.523:DA5.7-24)

And he saw a hand writing words on the wall, the cup in his hand began shaking, Judah looked frightened. His knee began to shake one against the other began and could not speak. Hadassah said said: what is the matter with you? Judah cried out loud, Hadassah look Elijah is hear, look he wrote on the wall, tell the kings to come and read the writing on the wall, the kings came one after the other and could not interpret the writing.

Hadassah said, do not let this writing frighten you I will send for Belhadassah, he has wisdom of the spirits of the other world he will interpret the writing. Hadassah called the horse man and said take some assistants an bring Belhadassah to me; they went looking for Belhadassah.

When they found him, the horse man said: Queen Hadassah want you to come to the palace. Belhadassah said what for, is there a plague in the palace? The horse man said its urgent, the new queen ask for you.

The horse man raced the horses on carriage to the palace, when Hadassah saw belhadassah she said I am now your queen mother and your father is a mighty God of the earth.

WHO IS GOD? HE IS GOD OF THE
SEED OF GOD. (DAN 2-47:4.17-18)

Belhadassah said: my mother, I had a vision and Elijah has made it clear to me God is a god of god in Hades, he is the father of God our father, no god is of creation, Elijah is created in the body of god after god sprit left his body for Hades. Without Elijah there is no hope for any god to have peace on earth.

BELHADASSAH FIRST KING OF MANKIND

Hadassah said, Bel this is your chance for you to be my king. Go and wash yourself, I will get some clothing for you to meet our God. Hadassah went through Judah's clothes and found a purple robe and sandals and gave it to Bel and told him when you are dressed come to the Passover feast

The trumpeter blew his horn and Bel came and stood before his mother and father, Judah said: Belhadassah I see you are clothed with majesty, I hear you have become a prophet to mankind and gods.

Judah said: There is writing on the wall I asked the Israelite Kings to interpret the writing on the wall and they cannot interpret this writing, if you interpret the writing you will be my successor on the throne

BETTER A WISE CHILD THAN A FOOLISH KING (ECCL4.13:HOS4.6-16)

Belhadassah looked at Judah (GOD) and his mother (Hadassah) Queen of Babylon. All the guests looked at him intensely, there was silence, he began interpreting, he said my God you have become great with your fear, killing the innocent to became a king, you made your mother your queen and abused her with your lust to make Israelites you did the same with your daughter and made mankind with her passing on the accursed seed and made her your queen, all from your seed is born in sin.

You made your daughters whore with giants and gods to make girls to mix and mingle with your mothers children, you knew Elijah is the Holy One created to save the kingdom for CHRIST to create Spirits,you imitated the devils who made gods with your mother and you made Israelites her and mankind with your daughter as your creation. You have no respect for me who adopted you to do good to have everlasting peace.

You have not humbled your heart and gave Belhadassah away from his youth, you forgot who save you from devils. I taught you scripture and skill you hanged Adam and blasphemed his Spirit CHRIST while you were King with the devils'

You made mankind with children with your mother sister's children, passing the accursed seed of god your father who raped your mother to make a god to be like him, you killed holy people on earth to replace them with your kind to live by the law of devils to Death.

The promise I made with you when you walked with me was before you took the oath to serve devils to be a prophet to teach gods to live by the covenant with Death, you did the same as god your father who had no faith and followed the devils doctrine to Death in everlasting fire, I gave you a free choice to rest in peace, you had no faith in salvation and not righteous to be my Son.

SIN IS UNTO DEATH

When you saw your mother instead of saving her from devils you chose to follow your desire to do like the devils to make mankind and Israelites your creation to pass on the seed of Death to destroy the flesh of your mother with disease with hate jealousy because you are not accepted above, you sentenced your mother and Eve and your children to be eaten by lions. You are not perfect and have many faults like the devils, all spirits from your seed that has no faith will be your inheritance in the gate according to the promise I made before you took the oath of devils to live by the covenant with Death.

You know the only way to be accepted above is through creation in the kingdom to live among Angels with eternal life, you have challenged me for the earth. Not by the power of Death with Multitudes of godly spirits you can succeed against me with the WORD,

You have followed the covenant of ancient devils with Death; they were removed from above the earth by the whirlwind to Hades by the WORD for raping holy women to make gods and giants and are awaiting final judgment to face with godly spirits.

You are worthless, all spirits from your seed will be ashamed to know you had a choice for peace and made them to be the scum of the earth to be carried by a whirlwind to Death because you hide the truth from them and make them think you created yourself, and you are mighty God who removed the devils to worship you to Death through lies.(JN.8.43-46:2: 2Cor4.4-12)

Belhadassah looked at God his Father and said this is the interpretation of the writing on the wall and all the guests began to cough looking at the mighty God the father of lies and Queen Hadassah in silence, Judah looked frightened the secret of the scripture he kept to himself had been reveal. Hadassah said my God you said Belhadassah time will come; (Jn8.43-45)

Hadassah said: what are you going to do? The writing on the wall has made everyone know you are a god born in wickedness passing on this accursed seed of god your father in Hades to them? Judah said the writing on the wall is the truth the Great Spirit is Elijah showing me his power, his way is justified to humiliate me for having no faith in him. I am a foolish King profane in wickedness with a useless law to rule all on earth with authority by the devils condemned to Death (Mal.2.11)

Judah beckon Belhadassah to him, he prostate, Judah took the ring Satan had given him after he hanged Adam to be a king and put the ring on Belhadassah's finger, took the gold chain from his neck and put it around Belhadassh neck and declared Belhadassah you shall no more be my forsaken son you shall be king Belhadassah third ruler after me and queen Hadassah with authority over the kings.

The ten kings came forward and lay their crown at his feet and wept for there mother and hated Hadassah who was ruler over them with her first son Belhadassah with Judah (God) there father, Hadassah said Belhadassah my sins with our father is passed onto thee to be king for all mankind.

Judah said Belhadassah you shall rule by my law to rule on earth with Israelite kings. If you have no faith as God you father your spirit will have no peace, make mankind, to populate the earth.

I will be with you where ever you go until I depart from the earth to the chambers prepared for me. Belhadassah replied I will follow you and my mother. All the guests said Cheers to the new King with the God of Israelites with his authority to rule and to do good for mankind.

JUDAH GAVE A SPEECH
(1PET.5.8.14:2COR4.2-12:JO8.43-46)

Judah said To the guests this is to let all mankind know Belhadassah is my first son with Queen Hadassah of Babylon, he will be accountable for his sin if he has no faith in the great Spirit that revealed the writing on the wall to show his power, he has a plan for all mankind who has faith in him to have peace as all from my seed is not perfect from generation to generation. The Great Spirit has reveal I am a father of lies and I deceived you by keeping CHRIST as my secret to populate my kind on earth.

Hadasah said, the writing on the wall has made all our guests know you are a liar, I gave you a wise son who is a prophet for the Great Spirit Elijah, give our king a palace in the provinces.

After the guests left the Passover feast the horseman took Hadassah and Belhadassh to the palace in the province. Judah remained in the palace in Babylon. He called for the harpist to play for him to sleep, he lay on the couch waiting for daybreak.

When he awoke he hurried to the lion's den and saw Eve and Tamuze and the children were sleeping among the lions. He was afraid to enter the den. He ran and called the guards to let the women and the children out and take them back to the harem.

The guards returned after bringing Eve and Tamuze and children from the harem to Judah. He said to the guards how come the women are alive? Let us go to the lion's den and he threw the guards in the den and the lions sprang on them and feasted on them.

GOD IS A JEALOUS GOD
(2COR. 1-13: GEN 6.4-5)

King Belhadassah and Queen Hadassah began going out together in Babylon when the people saw her with Belhadassah they would wave their hands and say, O Queen make beautiful children for your king, others would say you left the beast for Belhadassah, others would ask O queen is it true you left the palace of our God to live with your king.

A Israelite Queen said she is a whore she went with our kings, captains and merchants God our father is going mad he is crying for our mother and blaming her for leaving him for Belhadassah

Another Israelite Queen said to Hadassah our father is going mad and blaming you, he threw the guards in the den of lions and everyone is afraid to go to the palace if you don't go back to the palace father is angry and said he will kill you and Belhadassh he said he regret he made mankind with you all they will bring is his wickedness on earth.

Hadassah said Bel, if I don't go back our father will come and kill the both of us, he cannot do without me, Hadassah told the horseman to bring her back to the palace in Babylon. As she entered the palace, Judah held her by the throat, she was gasping for air, and threw her on the floor and said you are making an ass out of me with your king; I knew from birth the bastard would do the same and commit incest with you.

Hadassah began to cry: You beast; you fuck me like a devil. Judah got angry and tore the clothes off her and put her on his lap and started to spank her saying you are my daughter, you know you father has pleasure in wickedness you left me in this palace to go with Bel, he has bewitched you to commit incest, he gave her two more slaps on her arse

Hadassah cried; O God I love you, have mercy Judah said I will kill you, she cried thou shall not kill, she started kicking, crying in fear, saying O God, O God I will do whatever pleaseth thee

Judah shouted; this pain Hadassah I am suffering is for your absence I can bear to be alone without you it is unbearable I am a jealous God I am going mad, this incest with Bel is worse than all the wickedness I have done. I feel to strangle you for making me jealous to add to my sin, Hadassah cried. thou shall not kill I am under your spell, I will confess before you kill me. I am no good, I am cruel like you and cannot help this desire to have sex from my youth you chastised me to give you pleasure, you are a god that has pleasure in wickedness and have passed on your wickedness unto me, it's like a wild fire burning inside of me.

Judah angry and said, you passed on my power to Belhadassah now he is your king and both of you plan to make all manner of mankind on earth from my seed, I regret I made thee to be a sinner to bring more problems upon the earth with your whoring that is more than all the hairs on you head.

I thaught in my old age I would have peace with you, but you make my life hell every time you leave the palace I think you are not coming back plus all these dreams for killing innocent people to be a king. Hadassah all these dreams are terrorizing me when I close my eyes. Hadassah cried: my father, I cannot sleep with you, you cry and roar like the hungry Lions in your sleep and it scares me I tried to be good but I am corrupt like the devil that raped my grandmother now you hate me because I fucked with Bel: he is my king. You did the same with your Hebrew mother and made her your Queen to live by the law as long as you are alive, Belhadassah is my son, and you are our father, we are all corrupt, let me burn some incense to god your father in Hades to save us in the other world. Judah got angry and regretted he did not take Elijah's offer for peace, repent I made mankind with thee they will do the same and blame us for making them in sin. No matter how much incense you burn, there is no peace for the wicked. I will be punished because I knew scripture and had no faith to have peace, my punishment for blasphemy is more than I can bear and for spilling blood of the Sons of Adam/CHRIST for devils. to be a King

Hadassah said the devils are not among us now, what is the objective to carry on with their law: Judah said, It is to prevent Elijah and CHRIST from establishing the Kingdoms on earth and for all to worship me with fear of Death so when they are godly spirits they will fight with us for the earth. So comfort your God

Hadassah said I am tired, Bel is a prophet and know scripture like you with the Great Spirit Elijah let us go to sleep. Judah began to snore and cry in his sleep and shout Hadassah wake up, Hadassah said what is it? Another dream; Judah said a strong wind came and took me away and I was falling and saw a big sea monster with its mouth wide open as I was about to enter its mouth to enter its belly I had a vision and saw Elijah removing the grass from the stump of a tree and it began to shoot branches with a lot of fruit and the fruit turned into a lot of people and they began pointing their fingers at me saying he is the beast of the earth and others had a sickle in their hands saying let us catch the beast for Elijah to send him to Hades for killing our brothers, I began running in fear of what the devils will do to me. Hadassah said the spirits in the other world are after you.

Judah said: Hadassah the lions did not eat Eve and Tamuze and the Children; Hadassah said if you want me to stay with you let us put faith to the test again to see if Elijah will save the children of mankind, the Passover is not complete, you can't have two queens one going to heaven and the other going to Hades. It is full moon let us cast the children in fire as an offering to god in Hades. If Elijah can save them we will know he will save our children from Hades.

THE DEATH OF JUDAH

Hadassah said my God the spirits are after you let us cast the children in the fire as an offering to god in Hades I will stay in the palace till you return If Elijah save them we will know he will save our children to prevent god in Hades inheiting the spirits from mankind.

Judah went to the harem to please Hadassah. He took the last of his children born with Hadassah sisters to sacrifice them as a burnt offering to god his father in Hades. The women began to cry: king Judah is going to sacrifice our children to this unknown god.

Eve ran outside and tried to take the children from him. Judah shouted move away from me and my children; Eve said; why are you so cruel? What have the children done to you? They are mankind born from your seed by your daughters in this harem.

Judah shouted: They are mine and not from god you made with Satan he has passed on his accursed seed to me, they are not perfect like you. Satan strangled your god because he was useless and had no power like Elijah. So I am going to sacrifice them to him in Hades for not making me perfect, it's because of him all my children will need salvation if they have faith or return to Death. Because of your god I am cruel.

Tamuze shouted; Judah, you have become cruel since you took the oath to be a prophet to gods to live by the covenant of devils with Death. Because Elijah will not accept you as his son, you made children with me and your daughters to make Elijah angry.

As he was going to throw the Children in the fire, Elijah appeared in the flames and said: Ammon I called you when I adopted you from birth, Judah looked in the flames and recognized the voice, and in fear said what do you want?

Elijah said: I see that you have walked in ways of the devils and god your father in Hades for murder and rape, you have hanged the body of CHRIST and slay all his Sons and committed abomination with your mother that is forbidden in holy flesh and incest with your daughter to make mankind.

Now you want to kill the children you made with your daughters, behold a great plague will come and smite the whore you have made your queen in the palace and those you made with your mother you made Queen of Babylon.

A cancerous disease shall come unto your bowels, and you shall waste away day after day until your spirit have no desire to live in the kingdom from the flesh of your mother to fight against me with your godly spirits.

Your mistress you made Queen of Babylon has no desire for you anymore, when your spirit separate from the flesh of your mother, I will be waiting to send you to join the devils and god your father live to Death according to the law.

I am Elijah even to your old age, and execute judgment on spirits that depart from kingdoms that has no faith in me to save them from the flames in Hades. Your time has come to be without flash to plan your war in Hades against me.

Judah Cried O Elijah my End has come to be without flesh pray for me. Eve replied your mother and I told you to repent and ask Elijah for mercy to have peace. Now he has spoken the WORD on you and cant reverse it because you had no faith in him to save you.

Tamuze said why should Elijah reward you with peace, you agreed with what Satan did to me to make gods under oath, you did the same and made Israelites with you with much stress, you abused my body(Lev 18.13) and threatened to destroy kingdoms from my flesh because you were not born perfect and refused the offer of peace and made me to live under the law till you are dead, you held me in captivity like the devils to make Elijah angry with me.

When the time come Elijah will give me a perfect Son in creation by the WORD to populate the earth with perfect people from the Seed of creation to be accepted above.

THE MESSAGE (DUE. 21.28-23: 1TIM5.2-13)

Tamuze said, Judah when you get to Hades give god you father a kick for me for raping me to make a god like him to suffer in flames for his sin in forbidden flesh of my Father and Mother. Tell the devils I am free from there oath I am alive and made Israelites for you while they are flames awaiting the final judgment.

Judah cried: Before I depart from your flesh can you give me your blessing? Tamuze said you are accurse unto me from the time I conceive you in my womb, you will have Hadassah to bless you when you begin to cry for slapping me and stamping on my body for the Passover. She will curse you for making her a Whore in Babylon. The devils are waiting to baptize you in fire. Judah said I wish I had faith.

Judah returned to the palace. Hadassah rushed on him excited said, did you sacrifice the children to god in Hade? Judah began to tremble, could not speak, what happened she said you don't look happy? Did Elijah save them?

Judah pushed her aside with anger, Hadassah said, what has the witches in the harem done to you? My God and my King tell me what happened, Judah fainted, she put him to bed and told the horseman to take her to king Belhadassah. Bel said how is father, she said, O my king tell me what is going to happen father fainted you are now a wise prophet of a Great Spirit. Bel said God our father has annoyed a Great Spirit, he is disappointed in him for not doing good in the world and created confusion with his lies, no one know what to believe since he threw the guards in the den of lions, he went mad in the palace and everyone is afraid he will kill them.

Hadassah said, you are my wise King can God our father fight this Spirit and send him out of the earth, Bel said this Spirit is so strong he sent all the devils in the tempest to the fire in Hades,

Hadassah said if he is so strong there is nothing we can do, all we can hope for is peace so he don't send us in a tempest to be with the devils.

Hadassah returned to the palace, Judah was exhausted and fell asleep, the cancer in his bowels began to affect him he could not eat or drink and began to get thinner and thinner every day, his bones were protruding through his flesh lying in bed like a skeleton crying in pain feeling hot and cold.

Hadassah got a hand maid to lay in bed with him to keep him warm while she was in Babylon with her lovers

THE FOOLISH KING HAS SPOKEN, THERE IS NO GOD (PS 53.1: PS 14 1-3: REV13 6)

Judah began to cry don't leave me Hadassah with this hand maid, she make me hot when I am hot and when I am cold its terrible, she can't make me hot. Hadassah said you are the mighty God who created mankind in the world, command this cold to go away from you so I can see you have power if you can't your power is useless like the gods with a lot of faults, how can you save mankind from devils if you have no power to make this cold go away?

BECAUSE OF FEAR OF DEVILS AND DEATH, MANKIND WORSHIP ME AS THERE MIGHTY GOD TO SAVE THEM (REV13.13: JOB24.14-20))

Judah said: I created Israelites, with my mother. I am a king. Because I made mankind with you Hadassah the gods call me there mighty God. And idolize me with hysteria for making the feature of gods better than devils. Hadassah its Elijah I fear most after my spirit is separated from my body.

Hadassah said, before you made me your queen you said you did not know Elijah, why were you deceitful to me? I gave you the best of my youth, and gave you pleasure in your wickedness, why should I give up my lovers to look after you about to die, Judah said woe is unto my spirit when I depart from this body I have no one to help me.

Hadassah said, now you admit that you are a king and not a Mighty God who created the world. What is your spirit name so I can do witchcraft to contact you? Judah said my spirit name, it is Israel, when I go in the other world I will prepare a place for you and I so we can be king and queen of the spirits.

Judah said, if by chance we return to earth we will do more wickedness in kingdoms in mankind and seduce them to fight for the earth. Hadassah after I am dead embalm my body and take it the sanctuary in the tower of Babel so all on earth can come and worship me and you every full moon. We are not accepted and I can't save them but they can worship us. (Mt 13.1-58:1Tim3.1-58:Heb.3.7.11)

After this testament Judah said: Hadassah now I want peace, I am a foolish King leaving this life to go to Hades to suffer like god my father for wickedness, the pain of the cancer is unbearable making him mad, he began to cry, Elijah, Elijah, I cry to you. Do not hide your face before my End, come I am in distress, my bones stick out, my heart is failing me. I can't eat food I am reduced to skin and bones, my eyes close to see Devils, your wrath has come to cast me out of the earth.

Judah shouted for the scribes, they rushed to his bedside they gave him vinegar to drink to ease the pain, he said write this for future generations. People who are not of Creation may give praise to Elijah and have faith in him for CHRIST to come from Heaven for salvation of their body for their spirit to have peace.

JUDAH SAID TO THE SCRIBE AFTER AM DEAD MY SPIRIT NAME IS ISRAEL

Judah said to the scribe after am dead Elijah shall not call me Ammon anymore neither shall anyone call me Judah, my spirit name is Israel and have it written you are Israelites of God, then said great men in old age are not wise until they face judgment for having no Faith. (1IKi.17.3:Hos4.15)

Judah began to cry, O Elijah add time to my life, do not send me to Hades I am afraid of devils have mercy, your years continue from generation to generation on earth, don't let my spirit live my body in the presence of the scribes he cried In thirst.

The maid brought him some vinegar to drink and wiped his face Judah Cried loudly Elijah Elijah a voice came through the mouth of the maid; you shall not resurrect you will be sentenced 1000 years and you will return with godly spirits with no flesh from captivity to warn Israelites and Mankind if they have no faith in me they will see Death face to face.

As he was about to repent his body went limp to late to have peace. A whirl wind came and took his spirit Israel away to be in captivity a 1000 years.

YOU CANT SERVE TWO MASTERS
1JN.2.1-10: MK8.36

What good did it do for Judah to make Israelites and mankind to worship him as the mighty God and had no peace in the End. Babylonians never heard of CHRIST and ELIJAH. Judah kept the knowledge to himself as his secret for all to worship him as a mighty God self created and created the world.

Judah had no faith in Elijah who adopted him as a begotten son from the bush Tamuze left him after she gave birth to him for Elijah to save him from Satan eating him from birth,with salt.Elijah called him Amon and adobted him and taught Amon Scriptures and skill he had No faith and became disobidiant, and took action to be with devils to live by the covenant with Death for disobedience and deception to confuse all on earth to worship him and put their faith in him so when they become godly spirits to fight and destroy all flesh so the earth will be with populated with godly spirits to fight for the earth against Elijah, That was the plan of Judah godly spirit name Israel.

KING BELHADASSAH AND
HADASSAH QUEEN OF BABYLON

King Belhadassah had a vision of the Passover by Hadassah he saw the Spirit and Tamuz\e coming out from her body and was in the hand of Elijah and herd a lot of clapping praising Elijah for his holy work, I saw the Great Spirit in the light on his throne watching me and I heard a voice say it's the end of him who has knowledge to warn mankind to have faith in Elijah to rest in Peace.

Then I saw multitudes gathered in the tower of Babel putting the body of King Judah in the tower to worship him as God almighty. The Sprit Elijah in the light said Belhadassh you are living in troubled times in Babylon go and tell the people to have faith in me for peace before I make an example in Babylon.

Then I saw in the vision lightning and herd noise like thunder, smoke and fire and blood on earth and mankind was crying to God to save them but got no answer. Then I heard a voice say awake Elijah to begin Judgment don't let any godly spirit escape send them in captivity for the Passover

Then I saw multitudes carried away in a Tempest and they began falling on top each other crying for God to save them and they vanished, then I heard crying let us out from this heat we are dying of thirst let us out, they were the first godly spirits to be carried away to Hades from Babylon

Then I heard Salvation has come for Kingdoms from the flesh of Eve and Tamuze spirits that has faith will have peace and saw the Spirits of Eve and Tamuze Flying in the wind from fire then there was silence on earth. Then I looked there was no more holy people on earth then I saw multitudes in heaven giving Elijah praise for saving the Spirits Zion/EVE and Jerusalem/Tamuze from the fire to begin salvation in there Flesh to create New Spirits by the WORD, then I said to myself woe is unto me if I don't warn all the people on earth to have faith for peace

THE FIRST MISSION TO WARN ISRAELITES AND MANKIND (PRO4.1-19:JN.12.40)

King Belhadassah first son of God: He went to the province with Israelites and saw a rabbi for the Israelites. He said to them I thought it good to come and tell all Israelites about the signs and wonders that the Great Spirit Elijah has shown me

The rabbi and his Israelites said: We herd A Spirit is with thee. Belhadassah said: the the Kingdom is explained to me it is for creating Spirits to live the everlasting life from generation to generation and I have a plan for eternal peace on earth, it is based on faith in Elijah to be saved from falling to Death.

The chief rabbi and Israelites blocked their ears and said, don't trouble us with this vision for peace,you have dethroned our kings from ruling mankind and have taken their kingly throne from them in the nations

Other Israelites shouted, thou has lifted up yourself against God who made thee with his concubine who was his mistress and made her his Queen, now she is your queen, we dot accept this plan to change the law of God our father for faith in Elijah.

Belhadassh said: the law has many faults, the rabbi got angry, ripped off the gold chain from his neck God had given him after reading the writing on the wall and said you want to put division between Israelites and mankind. If this Vision is true tell Elijah to come and we will have faith.

The rabbi continued, it is written in the law that all who are evil will come after us, we pray to God our father to give us understanding. We are not like you brought up in bondage and lived among gods who deal in witchcraft.

Our father is a mighty God and his mother is our queen you hold in captivity, your mother is jealous because she can't make Israelites and made mankind for him so how can you talk about peace to us with a plan to have faith in Elijah who we have not seen or heard?

Belhadassah said, I came here in peace on a mission to tell you to stop worshiping God our father and have faith in Elijah for peace or you will be removed from the Earth for having no faith.

God our father had no faith in Elijah, he deceived us all on earth, rejected the knowledge of the scriptures Elijah taught him to have faith so he could have peace. If you are not willing to change our father's shame for glory in the kingdom and keeping passing on his seed, Elijah will punish who has no faith for peace. Belhadassah left disappointed

Belhadassh went to the next nation, the rabbi and his Israelites were waiting for him to discuss the peace plan in the synagogue: Belhadassah said to them I had a vision and salvation for kingdoms was reveal to me for spirits of Israelites and mankind that has faith in the Great Sprit Elijah can have peace after they die. It was reveal to me the kingdoms for salvation is for Spirits to be created in their image to continue on earth till the time came to resurrect to heaven.

The rabbi and his colleagues in the synagogue began to argue with one another then said we never heard of this Elijah it is not in the book of the law of God our father who created us from his seed with our mother who was his queen to be his peculiar people on earth and to be with him after we are dead to be his spirits to live by his law.

King Belhadassah said: God who you say is your father is the first god of you mother, logically speaking is your brother if he made thee with your mother. He also made me with his daughter who is my mother logically she is my sister we are all born in sin from his seed in the holy flesh of the Hebrew women and because of thyis we are not perfect we need Salvation for peace

The rabbi and the Israelites were silent and stunned at this revelation that God their father was hiding the truth, every Israelite was scratching their head and had no answer. Belhadassah said we are all from his seed and brothers with God. He is a god of god of the devil and wants us to worship him to Death.

King Belhadassah looked at the rabbi and the Israelites and said let us not behave like hypocrites for this is the hypothesis of the Truth, your mother is still on earth and can testify our God accepted the law of the devils under oath to live to Death.

The rabbi said God our father is dead with his secret we cannot ask our mother after we are dead he will tell us his secret to Death we shall populate Israelites by passing on his seed to be his people so he can inherit all the spirits of his people to fight for the earth with him, that is the promise by the law

THE PROMISE IS NOT BY THE LAW (REV17.6-7)

King Belhadassah said, Elijah gave God the choice for peace if he had faith for his kingdom to have a Spirit creation to be accepted before he took the law of devils under oath he had no faith to have eternal peace and took the law of the devils to teach gods to live by the law to Death this law is for devils to inherit godly spirits from the earth to destroy flesh with disease of Death, so there will not be any flesh to create Spirits by the WORD.

The Israelites blocked their ears started to scream no; no; no; now we know you are mad with this new doctrine faith for peace if Elijah appear we will have faith. Belhadassah said it is Elijah who brought up God our father from the bush in the wilderness. Your mother will testify God is her first god and Elijah adopted him as his begotten son from birth and called him Amon.

The rabbi and Israelites blocked their ears shouting lies; lies; lies; we don't want to hear any more of your lies, they started going out of the synagogue and saw queen Hadassah coming on her chariot with soldiers they began to run away

King Belhadassah went on his horse toward Hadassah. She said are they for faith for peace? Belhadassh said; my queen it's important everyone in the nations has a choice for peace, go back to Babylon.

King Belhasash went back to Babylon with this peace plan with much opposition in fear if they change the law of God they will be punished after they die. King Belhadassah was having a rest in his palace and had a vision. The Great Spirit Elijah said: Belhadassh, now you have kingly power over all Israelites and mankind in the nations, eternal peace will be unto thee because you have faith in me, now I will show thee what the Great Spirit CHRIST on his throne in heaven will do in kingdoms for salvation at the appointed time

In the vision I saw a Spirit in the light on earth in the midst of all kinds of people and a another Spirit in the light came in a whirlwind and went in the body of people all over the earth and saw godly spirits cast out from bodies and a whirlwind came and they vanished and left their body on the earth.

Then I saw the Spirit that was in the midst of the people taking the bodies that was good from the godly spirits that left the earth and they became people and the earth was populated with multitudes, and saw Spirits in the light wake up from sleep and they began to go above in the clouds.

Then I saw in another vision the holy Christ come from heaven and saw multitudes of people on earth and godly spirits was in their body I heard a voice saying don't let that anti CHRIST who blaspheme my name escape, save those that has faith in you Elijah the others are for God to inherit in the gate according to the promise you gave him before he took the oath of the devils to be a prophet, to teach gods to live by the law to Death.

Then I saw multitudes of spirits pulled up from the earth by the sun like dust to the gate and herd crying we thirst we want to go back to earth we can't live in this heat. I heard voices of devils saying we had a choice like you for peace but we chose to be sinners like you to make spirits for Death. Then a devil said you don't look like gods we left on earth we never seen your kind before are you Christ we never seen him, The spirits cried God made us with your gods and call us mankind and Israelites and the Spirit Christ cast us out saying we are Trespassers in the flesh of Zion and his daughters and He need bodies from their flesh for salvation to create Spirits like Himself in the light. Then the other Spirit that was on earth said God is in the gate waiting for his spirits who worship him to Death and has no faith in the savior of spirits on earth to join him and devils with Death.

Belhadassah began to cry; O Great Sprit Elijah this vision I have seen bring much sorrow unto me. I am from the seed of God in the gate I will end in everlasting flames of fire, I am afraid of fire, while I am a King I must warn mankind before they end in fire. Elijah said have faith and you will have peace. And your body will have a blessed Spirit created by CHRIST. So use your kingly power to save your people so they don't end in the Gate to be with God your father. CHRIST only accepts Spirit of his creation to go above.

KING BELHADASSAH GIVE THANKS TO ELIJAH (REV 19.20:14.9-11.RO1.25)

Belhadassah began to pray, O Elijah I thank thee for the vision of the End and the knowledge of Salvation which God my father kept as his secret from Israelites an mankind. He heard a voice answering, the Great Spirit said, Belhadassah I have heard your prayer. Now you have understanding of the End to send sinners that has no faith in me to fall in fire. My people are living Spirits in the kingdom living among you in troubled times.

I have used restraint on this evil generation, tell the people in Babylon the plan for all to have peace, God your father has deceived many and now the people of Babylon go to the tower of Babel to worship his dead body, who ever worship God, while they live in the flesh of the Creator, will have no peace it will be justified when Christ cast out godly spirits from his flesh in the time of salvation Elijah said, Belhadassah break off your abomination with your mother, minister righteous work, be merciful so the End of you as king will have eternal peace. None of your people have faith or have understanding of life after they are dead there is none beside you so tell them the vision of the End, so it is important to tell people in this generation of the choice they have to have eternal peace as salvation is far off, no one will blame you for not telling them the truth but blame themselves for not having faith.

Belhadassah told Queen Hadassah of the End vision for all on earth to have eternal peace if they have faith; Hadassah said: my wise king your greatness has reached to the heavens don't fail on this plan it is an opportunity to put this faith to the test so we can rule all nations.

She said I will prepare a banquet for thee my king for all wise men, merchants, astrologer, Rabbi of Israelites and seducers in Babylon to come and hear your plan for eternal peace on earth as salvation is far off.

Belhadassah said the Great Spirit made me his prophet and gave me visions of the end, now I have knowledge of salvation, at the banquet I will explain the way to eternal life is by creation of Spirits in kingdoms from the flesh of our Grand Mother. My queen we must change the shameful way we live by the law, adding sin to sin while we live passing on the accursed seed to make sinners in the flesh of our grandmother we will have no hope and suffer heat for disobedience.

God our father did not make anyone from his seed perfect we all have his faults. Salvation is for those in later generations. My queen the Great Spirit told me to tell thee to stop whoring to make children with different features as your creation or he will send your spirit to meet our father. He said you are doing the same as God our father to make all kind of children with you lovers to rule the earth as there Queen and mother. He said you have no respect for Eve and Tamuze and said you will have no inheritance on earth as all your children are born in sin.

Belhadassah said I will use my authority to do this holy work in Babylon for peace and who is not prepared follow the way of peace it will be there choice

QUEEN HADASSAH WHORE OF BABYLON

Queen Hadassah said: Belhadassah my wise king you have not had sex with me for the past 30 days, what is the problem with you, this faith mission has gone up you head an turned you off sex with me, or is it I who don't turn you on? Our father could not have enough me;

Belhadassah said, my mother there is a time to live and a time to die this passion to have sex will lead to Death. I had a chance to meditate on this incest with you and have decided to put a stop to it to have peace that is why I am not in your chambers, you have the choice for peace. Our father did not escape after he died in the palace, neither will you for slaying Israelite men and capturing there women to mix and mingle with mankind to make beautiful children to look like Hebrews

Hadassah said, My King I been chastised by our father to give him pleasure in my youth to make mankind for him and you are my first god and king I know no other way this passion for sex is not curable, if I give up my pleasure in this life and have no faith Ill join our father, be patient with me my son to have faith. I have prepared a banquet for all my lovers to hear your plan for peace.

THE BANQUET

King Beldadassah was preparing himself for the banquet, he herd a knock at the door, he said who is it? They behind the door said we brought your royal clothing from the Queen to wear for the banquet. He opened the door and they rushed inside and covered his head and stabbed Balhadassah and left him dead on the floor and escaped at the secret exit.

All the guests were waiting for King Belhadassh and Queen Hadassah to take their place in the Banquet, Hadassah came and sat waiting for her King, one of the guest gave a speech and said, Let us be joyful and give praise to our Queen for her new creation as beautiful as her to live by this plan faith for peace.

The old god who witnessed all the Sons of Adam and Eve killed said, what is faith since we shed the blood of the Hebrews gods have no peace on earth we are making gods for burnt offerings to the unknown god.

A giant stood up, said we are all brothers from the seed of devils with our Hebrew mothers and brought up to have faith,in1 God has put faith to the test and we captured the nations of the kings of gods and established their nations with Israelite kings. Another Giant said, we have two Hebrew women left on earth, and they are alive through faith, we should give King Belhadassah praise to explain to us this faith for all to live a long life in peace, our Giants are populating in the nations and get no respect for their strength and want to have a Giant King to rule in our nation in peace.

After much praise for Queen Hadassah for her new creation of Asians, the guests was waiting for King Belhadassah to come out to explain peace for all, there was much coughing and everyone was looking at Hadassah, she got up and went to Belhadassah's Chamber, when she entered she saw Belhadassah lying on the floor dead, she fell on his body crying and screaming: who did this to you my wise King.

She began to screaming; its treason; its treason; she tore the clothes off her and began beating on her breast my king; my king; who did this to you? The kings of mankind herd her screaming treason rushed inside and saw her on top of the body crying my Bel; my Bel; God you are a curse is this the way you repay me for making mankind? My Bel had Faith in Elijah for peace. Now I am queen of the earth without my king.

IF A MAN LAY WITH HIS DAUGHTER BOTH SHALL DIE (LEV 18.15)

Hadassah began to scream, I can't endure to see my Bel dead, he is my joy, she cried I have no wish to live, Ill kill those who killed my King, now the war for the earth begin. She embalmed Belhadassh body and put in the tower of Babel next to God (Judah)

THE TWO GODS SETH AND BELL

Queen Hadassah adopted two gods and trained them to serve her and her guests and was not aware they had desire to fuck her.

As soon as the cock crow in the mornings they would wake up, and come to her chamber to see what scraps they could find to eat, they began to argue with each other, its my turn to bath the queen, Hadassah shouted be quiet I am trying to sleep; She said Belial; you wash and soap my body when I wake up and Seth you will massage me with Lavender oil, shut the door and leave my chambers.

She woke up Belial prepared the bath and she entered and he soaped her body with fragrant soaps towel her and she lay on the altar of Judah, Seth began to massage her with stimulant oils, while Belial was watching, he joined in massaging and she began to say Ah; Ah; Ah; its good, Belial got excited and said O queen if you suck salt I will tell thee who killed king Belhadassah, she said ill have your salt but I would not like you to commit this sin on the altar. You have become perverted and want to fuck the mother of mankind have you no fear of me to be a mother fucker? Has my beautiful body beguile thee with base passion wanting to fuck the daughter of Judah on his altar.

If you want to be the first god to fuck on the altar of Judah you must tell me first who slay my king, if it's not true the spirit Israel from King Judah will come after you to make and End of thee with Death for your vile passion to suck the mother of mankind.

Seth said: O Queen if I suck salt I will tell thee who killed King Belhadassah? She said, Seth you can because Belial kept the secret from me. Seth said, while we were in the passage waiting for King Belhadassah to come and give his speech, we saw two Israelites with masks coming out from the chambers and they ran to the secret exit.

Hadassah screamed its conspiracy; conspiracy; The guards rushed inside, she told the guards take these two gods away and put their hands in the basket with vipers and don't let them go until they are dead.

Hadassah told the guards to get the workmen to gather much wood and pile them in a hip in the Palace yard for a burnt offering to God. She took her chariot to the city and invited the counsel in Babylon, Israelite Pharisee, Seducers, Merchants and her lovers to come to the palace to judge the Hebrews left for the Passover The guards went to the harem and brought out Tamuze and they tied her to the logs of wood, then brought a false witness forward he said; I recognize this Hebrew woman with two men who escape wearing mask, they asked Tamuze if she had anything to say? Tamuze said its all lies. I don't know anything about mask men.

The crowd shouted remove her clothes so we can her face, after they removed her clothes the once Beautiful Queen tied to a log of wood stripped naked looked old Another false witness came forward, said we were in the palace and saw these Israelites we had to see what they were going to do, after they came from the chamber of king Belhadassah they began to run but we could not hold them.

They ask Tamuze what have you to say about this testimony about your Israelites? Tamuze said no Israelite or god can condemn me if I have not done anything wrong, your witnesses are false.

The crowd shouted: Thou be of ancient days, the sins of your past have come against thee thou has conspired to slay King Belhadassah because of your jealousy of queen Hadassah who rule over thee, you did witchcraft to kill our God with disease

Tamuze said your queen Hadassah has gathered false witnesses against me, behold if I must die it will be for killing no one, I did not conspire to kill King Beldadassah, Queen Hadassah hate me and my Mother, she is cruel like her father who murdered the innocent to be a king.

The Pharisee and Israelites began to speak in each other ear, let us examine her more closely to know the truth of this Elijah king Belhadassah spoke about to have faith before he was killed. King Belhadassah said its Elijah who brought up God our father and called him Ammon, so how come his name is Judah?

Tamuze looked at the Pharisee then said: If king Judah was alive he would tell you himself, and if you have no faith you will be with him to ask him yourself and ask him also who is his father?

A Seducer said, O Queen Tamuze thou art waxen old in wickedness with devils and King Judah, you have sinned in the the begginning in abomination, If we condemn you is for making Israelites not perfect and making Mankind not perfect and for conspiracy to kill King Belhadassah

A Pharisee said to the seducer: are you going to condemn the mother of our God without knowing anything about her faith in the Spirit Elijah all these generations and where he come from and in what form he operate or his skill to keep Tarmuz and Eve alive among us with this Faith.

These men who killed king Belhadassah belong to a sect with much hate and should be on trial with them. The crowd shouted: we heard the witnesses is against her conspiracy in the palace, she is jealous of queen Hadassah the mother of mankind because she is not the queen of Babylon any more. The Hebrews are witches they made gods with ancient devils don't let them beguile us, they are corrupt burdened with sin let them be a sacrifice for the Passover to queen Hadassah to rule us.

The chief Pharisee said to the Seducer: we have searched the book of Judah there is no mention of the Spirit Elijah adopting Judah our God, we know he has the key of knowledge to the gate and kept it as his secret, there is No paragraph in the book in the book where it is writen faith will save Eve and Tamuze, let us set the wood on fire to see if Elijah will save them.

THEY WHO SHED TEARS SHALL REAP WITH JOY (PS.126.5:PS.78.1.8)

The crowd began to chant: Bring out the other witch who made a god for the devil its because of her the devils disappeared in the tornado, they had sticks in their hand to hit Eve shouting mother fucker who made a god to go in the heat for raping her daughter to make a god to look like him.

The guard brought out Eve she began to cry you are twisting my arm, You are hurting me, The crowd rushed at her and began to tear off her sack clothes and tied her hands back to back with Tamuze hands. The scribe went up to the log of wood with Eve and Tamuze and said what have you to say as your testimony for your sin to make a god to be a sinner, he has pass on the seed of devils to us. The gods say you were hungry and the devil gave you an apple to have sex.,to make a god to look like him? Is this true or false?

Eve said: I was ignorant like you knew nothing about devils and Sin, god of your father who you call your Mighty God passed on his seed to you to sin for Death. He did not have faith to stop this sin with the accursed seed in my flesh this I testify before you pass judgment on me, If I had you would be perfect and righteous in holy flesh.

I am free, and live under no law or commandments of ancient devils, every one of you with sticks and stones in your hands want to break my bones, stand in my flesh and want to accuse me of sin and not the devils who raped me to make a god and he has pass on the accursed seed to you. Any of you who is not born in sin can cast stones on my body until It is dead. When the crowd herd what Eve said they backed off.

Eve went on to say: when all of you depart from the flesh of the sinner if you have no faith the Spirit Elijah will send you to gate to ask your God why he repented he made you not perfect and to save you from the fire. This is my testament while you are standing in my flesh it is better you repent for calling me a sinner and have mercy on me and my daughter and set us free from being held in captivity to live in peace This you can write, I asked you to set us free to live in peace, If you want to continue to bring another sinner on earth don't blame me, blame the devils because you can't live in my flesh forever. And will face the judgment for being a trespasser in forbidden flesh. You bastards have no right to judge me or my daughter who has not sinned and want peace in this world for all who has faith.

THE TESTIMONY BEFORE THE PASSOVE

The Scribe said: Eve you have no witness to testify? Eve said this is my Testimony in your presence so you can pass it on so all on earth can pass it on to their children's children to have faith. After we are dead our flesh is our inheritance on earth for creation. Elijah did not spare the devils, and will not save any sinner. Queen Hadassah will be a witness at the appointed time for all mankind, Elijah has authority to build up and tear down, write this as a testimony for all to see who has no faith in him.

Hadassah left her seat, climbed on the pile of wood and gave Eve a slap on her face and spat in her face and slapped Tamuze and walked back to her seat.

Eve cried: O CHRIST you see what this wicked bitch has done before your face in heaven, I am bound with ropes with our daughter she is doing the same mistake as her father creating her kind to be there Queen on earth, your way is righteous and will be justified in the time of salvation

She is abusive and arrogant like her father and has no mercy,she blamed us for killing King Belhadassah with false witnesses as a pretext to set our body on fire for the Passover to rule as queen of the earth without your people.

CHRIST thundered: Be glad O woman, cry aloud you will have no pain like the pain she will have when the hour come she will not inherit from your flesh and Tamah,s flesh.

The scribe said: Tamuze what is your testament? She said: I am tied before you as a lamb for the slaughter I gave birth to you bastards you stand in my flesh and want to set my body on fire, I will be no more a victim but will have peace.

There was thunder and a voice said, there will be no peace while you are in your body. The crowd blocked their ears and said queen

Hadassah this two Hebrews live to hundreds of years among us burn them to Passover the earth to you, death don't seem to come to them put this faith to the test.

The Pharisee said: If we burn them there Spirit will take revenge on us and queen Hadassah and she will not rule on earth.

The Seducer said, we heard the witnesses say they will destroy Babylon for killing innocent people on earth. There was silence and everyone looked at Hadassah. Queen Hadassah went up to the logs of wood and said to Eve, from birth I was cast upon you by my father (Judah)

I am surrounded by these bulls that want me to be their queen of the earth, I am the daughter of God of your god because of him passing the accursed seed to my father we are born in sin and not accepted above and all who are here are angry, bitter with hate for holy people.

I am queen of the earth and am not accepted to go above just like God my father I am surrounded by these bulls who want me to be there Queen. I cannot be born again, I am born in sin and want all the their families on earth to know after the Passover you been good to Hadassah and told me to have faith for my peace. My sin has multiplied more than your one god who sinned to make my God who made me what I am a whore to sin for Death.

DAUGHTER IN LAW AGAINST THE MOTHER OF GOD (PS.76.2:48.11-12 MIC7.6

Hadassah circled around the logs of wood three times in silence, all eyes was on her, she stopped, looked at Tamuze and said: My father's sin with thee has multiplied and my sin with him has made all kinds of features on earth I am burdened with sin and am ashamed just like you Tamuze for what the devils did to my mother's mother who is your sister before I was born.

Your first god became your King and he made you his Queen. I did the same and made my first god my king, because of my father's incest and wickedness and abuse we both live under the law as long as he lived, he is dead and we are free. I sinned to make my king and he is dead, I deserve to be the queen to be among my people born in sin, our sin is your gain in the time of salvation after you Passover the earth to me you will be free I am a widow and will be queen among my people,.

Tamuze said you say you deserve to be queen among your people you should use your power to do good for your people, you have tied me and my Mother before all your witnesses and will not set us free to live in peace. I left the Palace when I found out Judah was my first god neither of us was compatible, I warned him I had no desire to make Israelites to add sin to sin they would not be righteous in my flesh because they are off the seed of god his father, he forced me to be his queen to live under the law till he is dead. I am free but you hold me and my Mother in captivity up to this minute and have no mercy and want to burn our body to make a name for yourself.

Judah said he repented he made everyone not perfect Gen 6.4 from his seed, if you set our body on fire you will join him in the gate because you don't have faith, Hadassah went on the logs of wood and hit Tamuze a slap on her face and said: If you and Eve worship me I will set you free and spat in her face.

Tamuze said: As you said there can only be one Queen upon the earth when I will be Queen the people on earth will be my people same as me. I shall not bow to you, you shall be in dust if you set these logs on fire, make the Scribe write this as my testament as your Passover.

HADASSAH SIT AS QUEEN THE MOTHER OF MANKIND (REV17.5)

Hadassah returned to her seat, she called the scribe and said did you write all what Tamuze said? He bowed and said yes your majesty. Hadassah said delete the name Elijah from the testaments so it is not mentioned for the people to put their faith in me from now on.

Hadassah called the Pharisee and Seducer and said, all of you in my presence desire for these two Hebrews to be burnt for the Passover for me to be your queen to rule all on earth, the crowd shouted burn them set the logs on fire so the Passover be remembered from this generation to tell their children to tell their children in the future the day the Hebrews became extinct from the earth and they Passover to queen Hadassah to continue with mankind.

CALL ELIJAH IN THE DAY OF TROUBLE (PS50.1-6)

The witnesses put the touches to the wood and it began to smoke and began to fire slowly with flames. Eve and Tamuze began to scream, in the smoke, suddenly there was one big flame of fire the heat was intense Eve and Tamuze screamed Elijah

Elijah save my Spirit, there Spirit left there body, Elijah held there Spirit in the flames, a wind came unto the flames and it became a great Light going upwards, the witnesses kept looking at this great light in the sky until it vanished from sight and they were in a tempest and it took them to Whykibuli a paradise island where there is everything exotic, many streams and rivers and waterfalls, thermal springs for spiritual healing, exotic fruit in abundance to eat, The Babylonians did not see their Spirit because they were still human, there body was the sacrifice to live the Spiritual life in the Light.

Zion looked above and gave thanks to CHRIST on his throne in heaven and the book of life in the ark in the tabernacle was opened with flashes of lightning written Zion and Christ live forever and there was much clapping, and praise angels saying Halleua Elijah Has saved the Queen of the universe. 144000 Brothers and Sisters in the heavens looked at Elijah and there Sister with Zion on earth and ELIJAH spoke the word: She is my Jerusalem the Queen of the earth and there was thunder and lightning in the sky and rain began to shower blessing on them on the island.

ZION THE PERFECT BEAUTY AND QUEEN OF CHRIST AND THEIR DAUGHTER SPIRIT NAME JERUSALEM

Queen Zion said: O Elijah thanks you protected me and saved me I am in your hands till I depart from the earth to be with my CHRIST. Jerusalem said: Elijah thanks you have saved me to be your Queen, My body was polluted with disease of devils there is none born without disease in my flesh. Thanks for your patience, while I lived under the law, it is excellent and wonderful to be with you in the Spirit.

I am overwhelmed I survived this fire to have everlasting life from violence and oppression in captivity all my life and to be with you in Spirit flying in your hand in stormy wind to this island. Elijah you have done great wonders on earth, saving My father and all my Brothers and Sisters to give CHRIST my Father the victory to establish all worlds with Spirits in the Light after Salvation of kingdoms.

Let my enemy lick the dust from under your feet to make the Passover complete to remove the accursed spirits of Death in my flesh, I want you to be my king as long as there is light in all worlds.

THE PROMISS TO JERUSALEM

Jerusalem said: Elijah all my brothers and sisters are in heaven except me on earth and I have no children with Spirits in the light in my flesh. Will you give me a Son by the WORD so he could pass on his seed to populate on Earth?

Elijah said: Jerusalem I will fulfill this with your Spirit by the WORD to have a SON and children from his seed will please thee and be our people on earth and you will be satisfied to be there Queen. We are Spirits and to do so you will have to Sanctify after you have taken a rest.

CHRIST decide when the work in salvation begin in kingdoms from the flesh of you, your sisters He will create Spirits to continue on earth to be his people by the WORD.

Jerusalem your Spirit did not sin neither did Zion sin you were in your image in the flesh with holy eggs to fertilize with holy seed to be holy people with holy Spirits like angels in heaven. The seed that is not holy is from Death. So the spirits that has no faith will return to Death and have no peace on earth.

AN EYE FOR AN EYE

For hanging the body of CHRIST and slaying all your brothers and raping Holy women to make gods CHRIST will remove every godly spirit from your flesh and return them to Death on the days of salvation

Elijah said Jerusalem, the time will come when you will have to sanctify to give you this Son, as you know the Kingdom on its own cannot bear Spirits to have heavenly life so this Son you will conceive with your Spirit by the WORD at the appointed time.

When there is no vision the godly spirits of God will perish because they have no faith or have knowledge of the choice to have peace and will end in the gate with God, Elijah said Jerusalem your flesh is your inheritance on earth and you will have to sanctify to have spiritual conception to have a Son by the WORD.

THE DEBATE AFTER THE PASSOVER
(PS 104.1-61K18.31-35))

Queen Hadassah had a meeting with the Pharisee and the Seducer in the palace she said to the Pharisee you shall minister the law of God our father to all on earth. The Seducer said. God made no one perfect in the flesh of Tamuze and Eve their flesh is their inheritance on earth.

The Pharisee asked the Seducer what will happen to the spirits of our God, we are his inheritance. The Seducer said King Belhadassah said before he was murdered God will receive all who has no faith in the gate according to the promise. Mankind in future generations will be bored with the law of God when they realize God can't help them when they pray to him and will stop worshiping him and do the same as us and have no faith and live in hope.

The Pharisee said, our mother was not ignorant she had faith in the Great Spirit Elijah to save her after she was dead, since she died everything carry on as the same with Queen Hadassah. The Seducer asked do you think Elijah will take revenge for burning the body of Eve and Tamuze in fire. Hadassah said they are dead we have put faith to the test, let us celebrate the Passover with the people so it can be remembered from generation to generation I am Queen Hadassah of Babylon the mother of mankind let us not discuss faith and uphold the law of God and live in hope for peace.

THE PASSOVER CELEBRATION IN BABYLON

Multitudes came from other nations to celebrate the Passover to Queen Hadassah and worship the mummified body of King Judah there God and king Belhadassah in the tower of Babel.

They washed themselves in the river they brought gifts to the queen and food and drinks, cattle, goats, pottery, and branches to wave to the queen. Queen sat at the tower there was long queues of people waiting to bow to their queen, the inhabitants were happy saying God bless our queen to rule over your people you created.

The square of the tower of Babel was full of people with little space to move outside the square there was music and dancing in the streets all over Babylon Trumpeters blowing their horns, flame blowers, artists painting. Butchers selling blood of goats cheering Queen Hadassah mother of mankind this celebration went on from day to and would at sunset

THE FIRST JUDGMENT AS AN EXAMPLE FOR KILLING HOLY PEOPLE

Elijah said to eve and Jerusalem you are Free Spirits with freedom, I have to leave you here on the Island, enjoy the peace there is every you need on the Island there is no godly spirits here to disturb your peace I going to Babylon I will be back.

Elijah got to Babylon and commanded the cloud to shield the sun and it was dark over Babylon, He commanded thunder, the noise was so loud the music could not be heard for the dancing in the streets followed by flashes of lightning one after the other, hail stones began to fall from the sky on the crowds and a stampede began people began crying: O God; O God save us and our Queen don't hurt your people.

Balls of fire began to fall from the sky and landed on the houses and fire began to spread from house to house by the wind, the people were running here and there trying to squeeze their way out to get away from the fire.

There was tremor on earth and Babel Tower began to loosen and fall on the people in the square, they began to cry. O God! O God! Queen Hadassah is in the tower save her. Hadassah could not find space to the exit, and was trapped inside the tower every one looking for a gap to escape fire, the wind blew the flames in every direction.

There was another tremor on earth and the Babel tower began to tilt and bricks began to fall on the people in the square there was no escape fire everywhere in Babylon multitudes burnt in the fire then there was a earth quake it split the city of Babylon in two and the Tower of Babel came crashing down in the depth of the quake with Hadassah and all the people imbedded in the ruble like a grave. (Rev17.9.20:Rev.17.5-6)

Those who managed to escape when they looked back all they could see was fire and smoke, the Passover celebration ended in desolation beyond repair, merchants and all who was wealthy was caught in the fall of Babylon.

After the fall of Babylon there was much clapping in heaven, Hail Elijah your judgment is justified, you have judged the whore who corrupted the earth with her father and for setting fire on the body of our Mother and Sister in Babylon, Make your next Judgment be worse than the first and sent there godly spirits to Hades for murder.

The third day after the Fall of Babylon the sun shined brightly, godly spirits began to come out of the ruble and was pulled up by the sun then a tempest came and took them away to fall in the mouth of the waters to journey to the gates of Hades to be in captivity.

THE BOOK OF GODLY SPIRITS FOR DEATH

The goddess in Hades took the names of the godly spirits that entered the gates of Hades from Babylon weighed them to see how much flesh they used and sent them to the chambers in fire.

Elijah is a Lord and Judge and where He is there is freedom, He returned to Whyibulli to be with Eve and Jerusalem after the fall of Babylon.

THE FEAST IN THE TABERNACLE IN HEAVEN

Angels from many worlds began their journey to congregate in the Tabernacle to worship the ETERNAL and CHRIST on his throne, Jesus and his brothers was on a building project for Spirits from the earth.

CHRIST said to Michel: take a space ship to the world of Jesus and tell him I want to see him urgently. Jesus arrived and went to see his Father, he said my Father you asked for me! CHRISTt said, how is the project coming on? Jesus there are many mansions to be built it will be ready before salvation begin on earth.

CHRIST said: My son you are always here with me, there is much violence on earth since the fall of Babylon I want you to take Genesis with your horses and go to earth. Elijah is on the Island Whykibuli with Zion and Jerusalem takes him up to celebrate the feast in the Tabernacle and to worship the ETERNAL Father.

While Elijah was speaking to Zion and Jerusalem, Zion looked up and said Elijah Jesus has sent a chariot of horses for you to celebrate the feast in heaven Elijah said what will you do Jerusalem after I leave you to celebrate the feast in the Tabernacle? She said I will wait on earth until you give me a Son to be a Spirit as us in the light in my flesh to give my father perfect children, Elijah said, I promise it will be so. Jerusalem said, when get to heaven say to my Father my brothers and sisters and the Eternal we love them and look for the day we will see them in heaven.

Elijah said, I promise it will be so, tarry here until I get back. Zion and Jerusalem and Elijah were waiting for the chariot when the horses arrived on carriage where they were on the Island, Elijah got inside the carriage with the horses and the horses began running on air to the cloud to meet Jesus, he got inside and Elijah and Jesus were on their way to CHRIST in the tabernacle in the heaven.

The news went around in heaven Jesus went to earth to bring up Elijah to celebrate the feast in the tabernacle. The angels began to line up the streets waiting for Jesus and Elijah to return from earth and they began to chant CHRIST! CHRIST! Blessed is CHRIST of the ETERNAL Father, who created his Elijah by the WORD, he sent the devils to Hades for rape.

The beautiful daughters of CHRIST and His Sons from the earth took their seat among Ark Angels in the tabernacle waiting for Jesus and Elijah.

Jesus and Elijah arrived in heaven and going through the streets on the carriage of horses to the tabernacle and the angels en route began to chant Elijah! Elijah! Hallelujah you condemned the devils and returned them to Death for abomination and raping holy people on earth your judgment is justified Hallelujah you judged the whore of the earth for setting the body of Zion and Jerusalem in fire in Babylon Hallelujah. Make your next judgment be worse than the fall for godly spirits who has no faith in you in the presence of CHRIST Hallelujah.

Mean while on earth the earth became filthy, there was none good on earth, Noah was a Israelite Pharisee he began to protest and was against the violent Giants his people crying, the Israelite men were killed and three women were raped and making giant children, he had a vision and saw spirits falling in fire and crying in flames.

Then he heard a voice in the vision, every valley will be filled and every mountain will be covered to prepare the way for salvation of kingdoms, the Pharisees have followed the shameful way of your fathers that lead to destruction. Noah was confused by this vision.

In his generation there were all kinds of Giants: mixing and fucking with mankind Israelites and gods in the nations and suddenly the earth with all sorts of Giants with different names Nephelim! Emmins! Golieth! and Annakins. There was draught and famine and shortage of food from nation to nation, the heat was drying rivers and streams and there was shortage of water, the earth was hot cracking because of the heat, and everyone was sick with all kinds of disease killing the Giants only the Anakins survived, the people blame each other for passing on their disease to them. Noah began to tell the people it is because of all their abomination, filth and rape they are punished, the end is near.

Secretly Noah began to pray to Elijah: O Great Spirit you saved my mother of my God in the den of lions, these visions I am having of the End give me understanding O Great Spirit my People are perishing, they have become slaves in bondage to Giants. They blame Israelites for all their troubles and don't worship God of Israelites.

They make a mockery of the law and call us unicorns and say it is because we burn our mother in fire there is shortage of food and water, O Great Spirit we need your help from all this violence. We are greatly diminished in population forgive us for our sins for our Mothers sake, spare us from this violence by the Giants who want to make us extinct from the earth.

The Giant ask us where is our God, if he is strong like Giants tell him to feed us and put food on our table, if he is a mighty God tell him to come and save his people from Giants. Noah said O Great Spirit save us so we can give you praise for ever.

Elijah said Noah, I heard your supplication, I will come and sanctify in thee by my Spirit to divide the spoil on earth, on the day I sanctify in thee I will cast out your unclean spirit and your spirit will have eternal rest, and your kingdom will have life with my Spirit to be in the presence of your people (Ps16.2.11)

Elijah said: Noah I have shown you in the vision what is good and what is required of thee to have eternal peace if you have faith in me to speak through your mouth and use your name, your family will Passover the earth to live in the kingdom until the time of salvation, the kingdom has become corrupt and there is no spirit that is righteous in the kingdom, Noah cried: woe is the sprits if they don't have faith in you. O Great Spirit let your Spirit Sanctify in my kingdom and let my spirit rest in peace and save all who has faith in you. Elijah said it will be so if they have faith in me.

Noah was in holy fear his spirit would be cast out form his body By the Spirit Elijah and accepted eternal peace and began to preach about things not yet seen to save his people, Noah condemned all on earth and began to preach all on earth is corrupt there is none good and the end is at hand. The Pharisees began to get agitated with Noah and his visions of the End of the world and said, Noah everyone is accountable for his sin an must observe the law of God of Israelites Noah replied if you don't have faith you will see the End.

MEAN WHILE IN HEAVEN

In the heavens all angels small and great took their place in the tabernacle gave CHRIST praise for fulfilling the testimony of the ETERNAL in the Ark in the Tabernacle. That his Christ will be a creator and will create his Elijah if the devils made a god and Elijah would cast the devils and there godly spirits to Death.

The voice of the ETERNAL thundered from the heavens of heavens. My CHRIST reign on the throne according to the testimony and has created Elijah by the WORD to fulfill the Testament in the ark before they were created what CHRIST and Elijah will do before he sit on the throne in the tabernacle to rule all worlds in the universe with angels in the Light.

The ETERNAL Holy Father blessed Christ and Zion and all angels of Christ from his seed and Elijah his first Son in creation by the WORD and With the WORD to do holy work on earth and blessed all angels he created populating the worlds with angels in the Light.

After the Eternal blessed every one, the Ark Angels came forward and bowed before CHRIST and put there crown at His feet saying Elijah is worthy to be King he captured the devils and resurrected you to the Throne of the Universe to create Spirits in kingdoms for Salvation on earth to live in worlds in the universe.

CHRIST explained to the angels the reason for the delay in populating the earth with Spirits in the light, and asked to be patient, he said after the Passover to the time of Salvation He will create Spirits by the Word so it will be as it was in the beginning without gods on earth from the seed of devils from Death. So all Spirits created can live by the new Testament to live in peace and harmony.

THE PLAN ACCORDING TO THE NEW TO THE NEW TESTAMENT (HEB9.28:13.8)

Elijah, Jesus and his Brothers and Sisters were in the palace with CHRIST feasting with much Joy, CHRIST was happy to see all his children from the earth was with him and became sorrowful for Zion and Jerusalem on earth.

CHRIST told Jesus to fetch the plan and bring it here. Jesus brought the plan. CHRIST said Elijah this plan is for you to build a vessel to Passover the earth to save the kingdoms that is good for the spirits to populate and multiply kingdoms for salvation to create Spirits by the Word to save the godly spirits that has faith to have eternal peace on earth to be justified and righteous.

CHRIST said Elijah you will build the vessel according to this plan to scatter the people you save all over the earth to multiply kingdoms for salvation So when I return to earth on the days of salvation to create Spirits to live among angels in heaven as my creation by the WORD.

Elijah every kingdom with godly spirits born in flesh of Zion and Jerusalem you save will populate godly spirits to multiply Kingdoms and will have eternal peace. And there children's children will do the same to make kingdoms to live to the time of salvation until I return to earth to create Spirits to continue in their image to be my people on earth to be accepted by The ETERNAL in heaven as my creation on earth to live by this new Testament which has made the covenant with statutes with devil obsolete. To give godly spirits a choice for eternal peace or return to devils to be Justified for there sin in Holy flesh ordained to make gods on earth to end End with Death.

SEED TIME (GEN.8.22: 9.1-17)

CHRIST said: Elijah let the people help you build the vessel so they may earn extended life to Passover the earth to multiply kingdoms abundantly on the face of the earth when the vessel is finished, let the couples you have chosen from all sorts in good health enter the vessel to multiply kingdoms for salvation.

After the couples enter, let the animals and creatures you have chosen enter, the gate of the vessel will close automatically. The wate will spring forth from all over the earth plus rain will fall to increase the water to lift up the vessel to Passover over the earth with people you have save to tell their children about the Passover.

The people you have not chosen, their spirits will be carried away to Hades to be held in captivity to prevent them from pestering the people populating the earth during seed time, after the Passover the water will recede and will return to where it was set to have a flow of water until the time of draught.

After the flood there will be a lot of water upon the earth. Blow the excess water to the south and freeze it to ice by the Word and do the same and blow excess water to the north and freeze to ice it will be a sign for godly spirits in the kingdom to prepare their kingdom for salvation when I return to Create Spirits for godly sprits that has faith to have eternal peace.

AFTER CHRIST DISCUSSED THE FLOOD PLAN WITH JESUS AND ELIJAH

After CHRIST discussed the flood plan with Jesus and Elijah, CHRIST sat on the throne among angels from other worlds, Jesus came forward and read out the plan, to flood the earth to Passover the kingdoms by righteous judgment on godly spirits to create Sprits in kingdoms for Salvation until there are no gods on earth to be as it was in the beginning with Holy Spirits created by the WORD in holy flesh without sin.

Jesus read out the testament by CHRIST the Passover by flood is to save the godly spirits in kingdoms that is healthy to populate the earth and multiply Kingdoms to Create Spirits in kingdoms for salvation by the WORD, it be Justified and righteous for Spirits created by the WORD to live in holy flesh of Zion and daughters CHRIST to be equal and enjoy the prosperity like all angels in the worlds. The godly spirits cast out from kingdoms Elijah will save those that are not Anti CHRIST and have faith in ELIJAH will have eternal peace and not end in fire to Death.

Jesus unveil the statue of Zion and Jerusalem for the Angels to see the perfect beauty of angels of CHRIST on earth, the angels began to cry for Zion and Jerusalem to join them in heaven,

Jesus said they are Spirits now and will be on the vessel in a sanctum built by Elijah to Passover to see the couples chosen by Elijah populate kingdoms in their flesh till the time Christ return to Create Spirits by the WORD to repopulate the earth with Spirits in their flesh for worlds without End. And it will be justified to hold godly spirits in captivity in Hades until the final Judgment for populating godly spirits in forbidden flesh of Zion and Jerusalem.

Jesus said the Testament of CHRIST is to give every godly spirit a choice to decide eternal peace in the time of salvation or return to the devils and Death in the fire until salvation end to the last seed of death in their flesh of Zion on earth to be justified by the WORD. This is the Testament of what Christ will do before the final Judgment on earth.

Jesus said to the angels let us give CHRIST my Father praise on his throne, the Creator of Spirits in kingdoms from His flesh on earth by the WORD with Elijah to establish the kingdoms on earth with Spirits acceptable by our ETERNAL FATHER with his blessing.

Jesus said Elijah is with us and will testify the godly spirits in kingdoms are doing the same as devils, they murder they have become violent and raping women, there is none good on earth they are all corrupt and will destroy holy flesh with disease of Death to prevent Salvation, judgment is in the hand of Elijah to save the kingdom. And do the work according to the Testament of CHRIST for righteous judgment on sinners.

Jesus said to the angels our ETERNAL FATHER has not shown his face from His heaven in the highest of worlds until CHRIST do what He is created to do to put the whole earth in order and create Spirits from his flesh to populate and enjoy prosperity in all worlds as his creation.

After Jesus was through reading the testament of what Christ will do to put order on the planet earth, Jesus said to the Angels the delay for final judgment is to give godly spirits a choice to have faith in Elijah to have eternal peace to end salvation for all godly spirits in the flesh of CHRISTand Zion to face the final judgment. The angels clapped their hands and said hallelujah woe, woe to who has no faith in Elijah Amen.

THE TESTIMONY OF ELIJAH

Elijah sat at the lower part of the Tabernacle and came up to the rostrum and congratulated Jesus and said CHRIST my holy Father you must let Jesus return to earth before salvation begin at the appointed time to confirm the testament of CHRIST before the Passover to save the kingdom and for people to tell their children about salvation to prepare their body, and have faith in Elijah who saved their forefathers in the flood to have eternal peace. Elijah looked at CHRIST on his Throne and all his brothers and Sisters from the earth and the Ark angels

Elijah said: It is a blessing to leave the earth to be among you in heaven to enjoy the perfect way of life and to have the plan to direct the kingdoms for salvation for CHRIST to create Spirits In kingdoms to live the Eternal life among you forever.

I am created by CHRIST with the WORD and I am with the WORD to do his holy work to save his holy Spirits and the kingdom, the devils did a lot of wickedness on earth to Christ and Zion and all my Brothers and Sister who are my witnesses in the tabernacle, I had to remove all the devils from the earth for rape, corruption, kidnapping holy women and burning their homes.

From these rapists there are all sorts of gods on the planet earth and they are rebellious and violent and enslaved by all kinds of passion like devils to make sinners to pass on the seed of Death, their spirits kill and rape and put much fear on the weak. If I did not return to earth there would be no flesh for CHRIST to create Spirits for the heavens from kingdoms from the flesh of Zion and Jerusalem.

I am Elijah the First Son of CHRIST IN SALVATION by the WORD. The plan to flood the earth is to Passover the kingdom from the flesh of Zion and Jerusalem that is good for salvation. And that is to save the godly spirits in kingdoms that is healthy to populate the earth with kingdoms for CHRIST to create Spirits in multitudes to give CHRIST the Victory on earth when all kingdoms have Spirits of creation and to end salvation forever in the Flesh of Zion and Jerusalem to be as it was in the beginning with CHRIST and Zion by the WORD to live in the flesh in their image until they are Spirits on the Throne in heaven.

Elijah said if I am in heaven I cannot do the work I am created to do and there are no Sons of CHRIST left on earth to populate on the Earth in Kiingdoms. I was created to do the work to save kingdoms for salvation and for godly spirits to have a choice to have faith to have eternal peace and not suffer torment in fire with Death.

Elijah said, further more Zion and Jerusalem has gone through much torment in captivity and humiliated I had to use extreme restraint from punishing the devils and waited until all the devils was caught in the act of injustice to remove them from living above the earth to Hades to await final judgment. The body of Zion and Jerusalem was burnt by the gods to Passover the earth to the son of god he deceived the gods after the devils were removed and worship him as God who created them.

Zion and Jerusalem are Spirits after their body was burnt in fire and have to wait at the appointed time to ask the godly spirits for mercy I am there witness on earth, and CHRIST and all my brothers and sisters will be there witness in the tabernacle at the appointed time to give full account of there life on Earth

The godly spirits are born in sin from passed on seed of devils of Death in the flesh of CHRIST and ZION, the only way is by judgment to return godlysprits from the seed of devils back to Death after they are judged fairly when CHRIST returning to earth to remove all godlyspirits from His flesh on the days of salvation. The angels in heaven began to cry O Elijah you are mighty with faith in CHRIST, save Kingdoms for CHRIST to create Spirits in multitudes to populate the worlds with Spirits to live among us in heaven.

ELIJAH ASK ANGELS TO HAVE MERCY ON ZION AN JERUSALEM

Elijah said, to the Angels when Zion and Jerusalem come to heaven have mercy on them, they will give you full account of what happened. The angels were shocked and cried we did not know there was problems on earth, all this rape by Satan and his Anak devils with hate and malice to make gods and Giants is abomination. The angel shouted in disgust Elijah let there be no peace for the wicked.

Elijah said: the flood on earth will be the opportunity to select couples of many sorts to save the flesh of Zion and Jerusalem as there would be no gain to destroy all gods and have no flesh For CHRIST to create Spirits in kingdoms for salvation so it's wise to save those that is young and healthy to populate on earth. The more they sin is more kingdoms they make for Zion and Jerusalem and at the appointed time to give Jerusalem a Son by the WORD to pass on his seed to give Jerusalem perfect Children in her flesh to live among the Spirits Created in Salvation to speed up the process to populate the earth with perfect Spirits for the worlds in the Universe.

Elijah said it is blessing to be in heaven, but I don't feel it is righteous to leave Zion and Jerusalem on an Island on their own there is none with holy seed to give them holy children until Jerusalem conceive a Son with her Spirit by the WORD with holy seed to give her perfect children on earth. Jerusalem have suffered and was kidnapped by devils to make gods and deserve to live in peace like every angel in heaven who was kidnaped by devils after they were cast out of heaven to make gods in her flesh. Zion and Jerusalem did not sin with their Spirit the devils sin is in their flesh to make gods to face Death.

After Elijah gave full account of life on earth to the angels of what the devils did and there gods did to burning the body of Zion and Jerusalem to Passover the earth for gods to take over the earth for gods to worship the son of god,they call him mighty God, he has challenged me with godly spirits for the earth. Elijah said this is a serious challenge against the WORD.

The angels began to cry when they realized the problems the devils left after they were captured and situation on earth needed Skill by Christ and Elijah to put the earth in order for victory and said Elijah mighty warrior of CHRIST it is Justified to flood the earth from all this violence and save couples to repopulate and multiply kingdoms for salvation for CHRIST to create Spirits in His Flesh and Zion Amen. Elijah returned to his seat.

THE TRINITY

CHRIST said with a firm voice: Elijah come here my Son and sit on the chair on my right hand, CHRIST said, my Son I create thee by the WORD with me to be a SPIRIT with the WORD in the Kingdom to serve me, the same way the ETERNAL created me in the Kingdom with the WORD to be a creator like Him to continue His work in creation.

Elijah you have commanded a tornado to come and remove the devils from the face of the earth to fall in Hades, and resurrected me to the throne in the tabernacle through your faith in Me to Create Spirits in kingdoms for salvation from the throne in heaven, Your judgment is righteous, you hate wickedness and deceit. You have my authority to go in and out of any kingdom to serve me kingdoms for salvation to create Spirits on earth. Today I consecrate you King in the kingdom, a Lord and Judge of all on earth by the Word. After announcing Elijah as King, Lord and Judge it was recorded in the New Testament.

The ancient Lords came and bow before CHRIST and gave Him their blessing and lay there crown before CHRIST as there was no need to have ancient kings in heaven to do the work according to the Testament what CHRIST and his Sons will do. CHRIST made his Sons Kings of their worlds.

The Ark Angels came forward and bowed Before CHRIST and Elijah for their work ended with the Testament of CHRIST what he is going to do before it happen and needed only Elijah with the Word to do holy work that is more superior by the WORD to establish order on the planet earth to populate the worlds in the Universe with angels in the light as His Createtor the ETERNAL HOLY SPIRIT by the WORD.

The Ark Angels retired from their work and to serve the ETERNAL in the highest world for CHRIST to do what He was created to do to rule and have dominion in all worlds with Angels of Creation. He was angry Zion and Jerusalem had to wait on earth for the Passover to inherit their flesh for Salvation. CHRIST said to Elijah you are my rock and put my faith in you with the WORD to deliver the work with the Spirit of the wind, thunder, hailstones, thunder, balls of fire, lightning, earthquakes, fire, rain, flood, to put an End to sin in the flesh of Zion and Jerusalem to the last seed of Death.

Elijah became King, Lord, Judge, of godly spirits in kingdoms in all nations on earth to give CHRIST the Victory. The angel began to sing Elijah mighty Son of Christ, let your second judgment begin with the flood for eternal redemption, have mercy and save couples to be in the vessel to testify to their children you saved them and to put their faith in you for peace. CHRIST and all his Sons and Daughters and angels blessed Elijah and told him to give Zion and Jerusalem there love and peace.

The angels returned to their worlds there to live by the new Testament of Christ with confidence in Christ to remove sin in the UNIVERSE and for all his creation to be equal and enjoy the prosperity in the worlds. To rule with Zion and have dominion in all worlds in the universe when she is on throne in heaven.

THE FLOOD TO PASSOVER THE EARTH
(ESSEK !4.17-18. 1PET3-20)

The time has come for judgment some will be chosen to Passover from multitudes in the flood.

Elijah returned to earth to begin the construction of the vessel, the spaceships brought the necessary equipment for the vessel, panels, machinery, panels, nails, screws, bolts and satellite navigation to speed up the building of the vessel and spaceships returned to the heavens.

Elijah sanctified in the body of Noah and cast out his spirit to have everlasting sleep. The body was now made perfect with the Spirit Elijah. That is to say the spirit of Noah exist no more in his body. Elijah can now use Noah's body speak the WORD through the mouth of Noah walk use his hands and no one will Know the difference when he is building the vessel.

The population of the earth was two hundred million people in that generation scattered in the nations on earth after the fall of Babylon. Elijah started clearing the place cutting down trees in the forest with his chain saw and moving the logs with caterpillar. The falling of trees made a lot of noise attracted a lot attention and people came and asked, Noah what are you doing? Are you crazy; clearing all this forest and they began to laugh and went to tell the Pharisee Noah is clearing the Forest?

The Pharisee came to the forest and said: Noah you are not following the tradition of God our father, you do things like the gentiles who don't care for the Law of our God, stop clearing the forest or I will report you to the local rabbi in this area to stop you.

The rabbi came with other Pharisees and seducers, Elijah said through the mouth of Noah, did you come to do battle with me? Or did you come to collect taxes? If you don't get what you want you kill or rape who don't pay.

A Pharisee said, it is against the law to build in the forest of our God, if you don't stop this we will get our Giant Anakin to destroy your machinery, Elijah said I am building a vessel for the holy CHRIST in heaven. Many people gathered and said Noah when we ask God for anything he don't give us, Noah said it is because they don't ask Christ in heaven and hate the good Spirit Elijah, He has given grace to the body of Noah.

Elijah opposes the proud and gave grace to Noah. The Pharisee answered. Noah Elijah is against the Law, Elijah/ Noah, said there is one Lawgiver and there is One Judge who can save and destroy.

You come here and tell me I can't build a vessel for CHRIST, and don't know if you will live tomorrow or where your spirit will end, you brag and boast about the Law of God, you live in comfort and come to the forest and tell me to stop working on the vessel I am going to build for Christ in the forest to give work to those who want work to feed their children.

The Pharisee and the rabbi said Noah/Elijah why do insist to build this vessel do you want to start a revolution in the forest with workers? We are going to get our strongest Anakin to destroy all your machinery so you don't build this vessel for Christ and Elijah.

Elijah/Noah said if God is your rock let us put God to the test to see if your strongest Anakin has power to prevent me from building this vessel for Christ; the crowd started to shout at the Pharisee and rabbi; We pray to God to put food on our table to feed our children, he never respond, our children are sick dying with disease and hunger, our old are sick and there is no bread in the nation and you and your giants come and collect tax to live in the nation

Elijah/Noah told the crowd to come and stand before me, if any of you believe God made the world stand by the Pharisee and the rabbi and ask them to pray to God to feed the children standing here with bread, and those of you who don't believe God can't deliver stand by me.

The Pharisee said Noah/Elijah you want to bring division in the nation to break the law of our God.

Elijah/Noah said; God has no power and the law will lead many astray from the truth, let us put God to the test against Elijah and see if God can feed the people standing next to you with bread? If God can feed the people with bread he has power more than Elijah.

If Elijah can feed the people next to me with bread, Elijah has more power and he can build the Vessel in the forest.

The people who stood next to the Pharisee started to argue and saying to those next to Elijah/Noah, traitor our God will punish you for following Noah, both sides blaming each other for the problems on earth with violence, murder, and rapist in the nation by Giants. Elijah/Noah kept his cool as both sides began shouting at each other.

The Pharisee said, God will punish every one of you in the forest if you back Noah to build the vessel. The party next to Noah/Elijah shouted if God can feed us with bread let it come from the sky now and we will have faith in him.

Elijah/Noah said to the crowd: all this violence and abomination and religion with laws and commandments lead to Death if God don't show you his power today.

The Pharisee and rabbi was furious at Noah/Elijah said Ok you will see who has more power and began to pray; O mighty God show your power to Noah and the people next to him, make bread come from the Sky? The Pharisee and rabbi got no response from God.

Elijah/Noah said to the Pharisee and rabbi I am going a stone throw from you and command bread to fall from the sky to feed everyone here to show you the power of Elijah on earth.

The sun shone bright on the body of Noah. Elijah lifted the hands of Noah towards heaven and commanded bread to fall from the sky. The people picked up the bread and brought it to Noah/Elijah and said rabbi Noah is our Prophet, Elijah has chosen Noah to put the Pharisee and rabbi to shame today

Noah/Elijah, said to the Pharisee and Seducers if they want to put God to the test to see if he has more power than CHRIST on the throne in heaven? the Seducer said, there is no CHRIST in heaven, our God made the world and we are his children and he has authority over all his children on earth.

Noah/Elijah said to the Pharisee and Seducer it is true you are children from his seed of God of god, but his children live in the flesh of CHRIST and He has power to cast out all sprits of the children of God from His flesh for God to inherit when CHRIST come to earth from heaven. CHRIST in heaven can show you what God cannot do before your eyes to witness his power from heaven?

The Pharisee and Seducer said Noah there is no CHRIST nothing is written about this CHRIST these Visions you have will bring division on earth, no Christ exist if you want to put this CHRIST to the test against God we will laugh at you if He don't Show his power from heaven you can't build the vessel in the forest.

Noah/Elijah said to the Pharisee and Seducer, get the strongest Anakin Giant to get logs of wood and pile it up on your side, and I will get the people on my side to pile logs of wood on my side, so there will be two piles of wood, the pile on your side you call it Hadassah and the other pile on my side I will call Eve and Tamuze.

CHRIST AGAINST GOD

Noah/Elijah said to the Pharisee and Seducer. Look there, are two bulls you take one and kill it and chop it in tiny pieces and put it on the on the pile of wood on your side and throw the blood on the pile for all the violence, disease, rapists, and disorder on earth.

Noah/Elijah said, the people on my side will kill the other bull and chop the meat in small pieces and put it on the pile of wood and throw the blood on the wood for all on my side for CHRIST to heal the sick in on my side from disease in his flesh.

FAITH IN CHRIST OR FAITH IN GOD IS PUT TO THE TEST

Noah/Elijah said to the Pharisee and Seducer, you are indoctrinated with the religion of Judah who call himself before he died the Mighty God who created you pray to him and tell him to set the pile of wood on fire to heal all the people on your side from disease he has more power than CHRIST in heaven.

The Pharisee and Seducers and those on their side: O God our father set the logs of wood our side and heal your people who is sick on our side and burn all the flesh on the wood to ashes to show Noah your power and his faith CHRIST in Heaven is useless vision to corrupt and cause division on earth.

This contest gathered many in the nation saying the Spirit of Elijah is with Noah he is our prophet now he made bread come from the sky

The Pharisee and seducer and the people on their side to pray, O Mighty God show Noah your power, he is a delinquent and backslider and want to start a revolution in the forest, show them you have power to heal the sick and set wood to the fire to burn up all the flesh in fire. To ashes, we have faith in you o mighty God. They got no response.

Noah/Elijah said; May be God is fast asleep shout louder, they began to pray louder and louder, they blew their horns, wake up O Mighty God, they began to cut their arms, legs and face blood dripping falling on the earth crying O God show Noah the son of a bitch born in abomination, and all his delinquents your power and heal your people that has faith in you on our side. Once again they got no response.

Noah/Elijah said to the Pharisee and Seducer, you have this day chosen who you have faith to save you after you are dead, and said to the people watching this contest of faith to come closer, Noah/Elijah looked at them and there was silence, and said hear me each of you gathered here today and let it be known. Elijah is the Son of CHRIST in Heaven, A Lord and Judge of the whole Earth, then turned to the Pharisee and seducer and said you have began to show anti CHRIST on earth with the law to mislead to mislead people to Death.

You have made yourself foolish with laws of ancients devils neither do you have faith in Elijah who fed the people in this nation with bread from the sky, when you are dead you will see if God can save you.

Noah/Elijah told the people who stood by him to get buckets of water and throw on the flesh of the bulls on the pile of wood, blood and water was around the wood, then looked at the Pharisee and said this is how it will be for people to see in later generations on One innocent who has faith suffering by one like you who has no faith from Hades.

CHRIST ANSWER BY FIRE

Noah/Elijah said before the crowd, CHRIST make fire come from heaven set the logs of wood on fire to show everyone your power in heaven and earth and can do what God cannot do earth and heal the people on my side from disease.

Suddenly there was darkness and lightning came from the sky on the logs and set the logs with meat on fire and the fire began to burn the flesh with devouring fire on the blood and water with nothing left but scotched earth and all who were sick were cured to work on the vessel. The people was afraid, Noah/Elijah commanded the Anakin Giant to take the Pharisee and Seducer to the valley and slay them for having no faith and leading the people astray with the law and return to help him build the vessel according to plan with Testament in the Ark what Christ and Elijah will do on earth.

The people in that generation witnessed putting God to the test he did not respond to the supplication of those who worship and live by the law and saw those who stood by Noah/Elijah saw what Elijah and Christ could do what God could not do. It was beyond the imagination of those who lived in that generation to know Elijah was sanctified in the body of Noah and was among them with the WORD. The Pharisee and Seducer did not know what to make of Noah they thought Noah was mad putting God to the test. The name of CHRIST and Elijah was removed from their book.

Elijah/Noah began to clearing the up the sight in the forest to set up the vessel, the people asked him for work to help clear up the forest. They looked upon Noah as a Prophet and revolutionist with knowledge and wisdom and had faith in the Great Spirit Elijah and made Noah there Prophet.

THE CONSTRUCTION OF THE VESSEL

Length 167.7m, width18m, height 27m, built with lower deck, second deck and third deck, decks fitted with potholes. On top of the vessel the sanctum for Zion and Jerusalem with made of gold.

The vessel was fitted with solar batteries to propel the vessel, navigation by satellite system, kitchen for cooking, air conditioning to regulate the temperature in the vessel and preserve plants, two statues with outstretched wings with many colours one fitted at the bow of the vessel and the other fitted at the rear of the vessel, in the Ark was the scroll the copy of the Testament of Christ inside.

The vessel was fitted stalls for beasts, cattle sheep and goats, cages for birds and insects, creatures, and fruit cuttings and seeds of various plants and herbs

Every morning the people who worked would collect their bread, Partridge and quail fallen from the sky in a part of the forest. The people lived on site working on the vessel.

The Pharisees and astrologers from other nations came on site and said to the Giant Anakin who gave you the right to kill our brothers who do the work of God in this nation? The Giant said why can't God do his work and need your brothers to do his work and force people to live by his law. Noah Put God to the test and he did not respond, the law is of ancient times and put fear in the people and no hope we are working, we have food to eat and we are in good health.

The workers on the vessel shouted at them, we are satisfied we eat bread, and roast the partridge and quail that come from heaven, what is it with you, go away with your Law. The Giant Anakin said if you don't leave I will break your neck in the forest, the Pharisees began to tremble and cry don't break our necks, we herd Noah put God to the test and we want to know about this Spirit Elijah with Noah who made fire come from heaven to set the wood on fire, we were told by our witches they saw in a crystal ball the Spirit Elijah is with Noah and we want Noah to tell us about this Spirit that is not known, there is a lot of violence, murder and rape among our women and we want Noah to make contact with the Spirit Elijah to save us from these Murderers of the seed of ancient devils

The Pharisees said we know God did not make us perfect and we are his peculier people with many faults. we are diminishing in population because of these violent rapists and murderers killing our people we came to ask Noah to ask this Spirit Elijah to save us from these Barbarians of ancient times.

Noah/Elijah said if you were perfect you would not be on earth it is your people who Burn the last two good People on earth for the Passover to do the work of God? Why do you want the Spirit Elijah to save your people if they are not perfect? The Spirit Elijah save who has faith in him, like all you see working on the vessel for a better life.

The Giant said, Rabbi we don't believe God has more power than the Spirit Elijah also he has a back up Spirit name Christ in heaven who set the wood on fire with meat and blood and water and heal us from disease and we are not hungry we are building this vessel for CHRIST because he has shown his power to set the wood on fire from heaven.

The astrologer said, Noah we see the sun moon and stars above but we have never heard of Elijah and this Spirit CHRIST to teach our children about their power to have faith in them, this faith you are talking about is a new religion. We were brought up by our parents to worship our God until we are dead.

Noah/Elijah said the reason why you don't know about CHRIST and Elijah is because your religion writers in Babylon were seduced by demons to put a lot of …. where CHRIST and Elijah is mentioned to lead many to Death, to brain wash many to worship God and use the Law of ancient devils and put fear of Death to collect taxes to hide the truth of what CHRIST and Elijah will do for killing holy people on earth.

The astrologers and Pharisee began to argue about this new doctrine of faith and said Noah we think it is you who is brainwashing those who are building the vessel with the Spirit Elijah, for this CHRIST, you are mad how can this vessel sail in a forest if there is no water, when the vessel is finished don't come to the synagogue to cry to us to let you in and ask for mercy, we will laugh at you for abandoning the Law of God for this Faith in this Christ and Elijah.

Elijah/Noah said, the wisdom in this generation is crafty and use this foolishness of the law that cannot save no one that has no faith and will see who is the judge of the earth when the vessel is lifted from the forest with those who has faith, don't cry to let you in when the door of the vessel is shut, this will be opportunity to put God to the test to save you when the vessel is risen. Elijah said through the mouth of Noah judgment is long overdue to this generation (2Pet14.2) every valley shall be filled with water, every mountain covered with water to prepare the way for the generation saved to populate the earth making Kingdoms for Salvation (Lk3.4)

The Pharisee and Seducer and others began to laugh, Noah you are mad, this vessel will never sail from this forest, could not stop laughing Noah The Spirit Elijah has made you mad and they left,

PREPARATION FOR THE PASSOVER OF THE EARTH

The vessel was now finished and the workers made carpets for the interior for the 2nd and 3rd decks, some gathered seeds, others gathered cuttings from fruit trees and various plants and the workers began to carry everything inside the vessel to the cool rooms to keep fresh.

The news went round in the nations the vessel was finished and all sorts of people came to the vessel and wanted to come aboard, there was a long queue and they had to strip naked to go through health check to make sure they had no blemish of any kind or disease. Every male and female and their children that was accepted had to take a deep in the pool of water to remove all dirt from their body and went inside the vessel on the 3rd deck.

The couples accepted had to go to the same procedure to strip for heath check to a deep in the pool and went inside the vessel on the 2nd deck and 1st deck in all 6000 people on the vessel.

They that were not accepted were angry and shouted abuse at Noah and telling the people to get out Noah is mad he will kill every one of you inside the vessel when the gate is shut.

The door of the lower deck was opened there was a stampede goats, sheep, from everywhere began heading for the vessel, fowls dogs cats creatures and insects and beasts rushing to get inside the vessel taking up every space and the gate was shut automatically.

The sun went in a cloud and suddenly there was darkness all over the earth, lightning and thunder with loud noise that was never heard before continuous lightning and earthquakes. Elijah caught the jet stream to Whykibuli to meet Zion and Jerusalem; they returned by jet stream to the vessel and went to the sanctum on the top deck.

THE FLOOD

The earth began to tremble and fountains of water from the deep began spouting water everywhere on earth plus heavy rain falling continuously, there was water everywhere the people began to run to high ground, rain and water from the fountain brought flooding and began to run up hill crying O God save your people, they got no response

Water began running down mountains and fill up valleys and came unto the vessel in the forest it started to creek taking the strain, it moved sideways and suddenly the vessel began to rise upwards in the same ratio with the water. The people began to shout open up Noah so we can get in to be with the beasts. Others cried we are going to die let us inside the vessel, but the vessel was too high to climb to hitch a ride.

The people began running on top of hills to escape, they began to cry to the Pharisees. The End has come for multitudes of the family of God we will all die in this flood we have made the Great Spirit Elijah with Noah angry with us, slowly the water was gaining height on hills and valleys were filled.

Multitudes who tried to stay afloat among beast and snakes died, bodies floating everywhere on earth, slowly they began moving upwards to the peak of mountains and the vessel prevailed sailing over the planet earth, no earth could be seen in victory over Death.

The multitudes that died, there spirits in the flood was heading to the gate of Hades and when the last spirit entered the gate was shut automatically to be in Hades for 1000 years to stop them from pestering the people chosen by Elijah to live in peace on earth to make kingdoms for salvation.

The rain and water from the deep stopped, the vessel drifted in silence in calm water Elijah went among the people and animals to see they were alright. Zion and Jerusalem saw the Passover and multitudes dead in the flood.

A TESTAMENT IS MADE BEFORE PEOPLE ARE DEAD

The People saved can testify to their children they witness multitudes died in the flood and was saved by the Spirit Elijah with Noah in the flood in the Passover to begin a new life on earth according to the Testament in the Ark on the vessel to populate the earth to make kingdoms for salvation for CHRIST to create Spirits. The mystery of the ages is written.

Elijah said to the people in the vessel: it is good to bear witness to multitudes that died in the flood who followed religion with laws and commandments to live to Death contrary to the Testament in the Ark for all saved to live and have faith in Elijah to save them from Death for everlasting peace

Because you have faith in Elijah you worked on the vessel, you were fed with bread from heaven and now resting in peace in the vessel because of your faith to start a new life to populate the earth to make kingdoms for salvation for CHRIST in heaven to create Spirits in perfection to be accepted in heaven in the time of salvation, so don't go back to your old way and worship God to Death as you saw multitudes dead in the flood.

When the earth is populated in multitudes your children will have the same free choice to have faith in Elijah to save them for their spirit to rest in peace. The flood is the beginning to learn to have faith, and to tell your children to tell their children to prepare their body for salvation to have a Spirit of creation to live the everlasting life for their spirit to rest in eternal peace. Elijah said it is wise you all are gathered in the vessel, hold on to faith, and always keep your body clean and healthy so your children will do the same so they do not spread disease to destroy flesh. Through the mouth of Noah Elijah spoke to all he saved, as godly spirits in there humanity can't see a Holy spirit while they alive in the kingdom.(1Pet4.6-17)

Elijah said to the people in the vessel every one of you is accountable for his action and must teach your children and tell them the truth before CHRIST return to earth in the time of salvation to create Spirits to be righteous in the kingdom.

After Elijah explained his reason for the flood, the people began to sing. Elijah saved us, we have seen his judgment and we will testify he saved us and saw multitudes dead in the flood to live on earth after the flood till salvation.

A Israelite said uncle Noah our father wrote Genesis, could you tell me the truth about the serpent and the apple? Elijah said his mother called him a serpent because he beguiled her to marry him under the law to make Israelites and did not tell her the truth he was her first god, that is the reason why you are not perfect and in the vessel so bring up your children to Know the truth and to have faith to have eternal peace. God is angry he is not a creator and did not make anyone perfect so have faith it is good you want to know the truth.

A woman said: I had a dream and I saw a Great Spirit in the light as bright as the sun come from heaven and began to cast out spirits from bodies. Then I saw a Great Spirit in the light waiting for the spirits cast out from bodies, and a tempest carried them away and they vanished.

Elijah/Noah said the Great Spirit you saw casting out the spirits from bodies is CHRIST from heaven coming from heaven to create Spirits in the body of your children to continue on earth. It is important you ask questions to know the Truth while you are in the vessel to know what is required on earth is for all on earth to be of creation to live long life on earth in peace and prosperity until there time come to go to heaven.

Elijah/Noah asked the people, do you understand the purpose why you are saved in the Flood? The people answered yes. Hallelujah Elijah extended our life to populate the earth for CHRIST to create Spirits in kingdoms for salvation.

THE SANCTUM ON THE HIGH DECK OF THE VESSEL

After speaking to the people of what is required, Elijah entered the sanctum. Zion said Elijah you are always working. Elijah said I look for the day when the work is complete to the last seed of Death in your flesh to be free of sinners, it is important the people know the choice they have so they don't do the same mistake as Judah to live to Death in the final judgment, the dead in the flood is for them to warn their children to have faith to have eternal peace In the time of salvation. They tend to go back to the ancient way and make gods in their imagination to worship to do evil on others to lose faith. Elijah said Zion you have one more Passover to go through and you will be on your way to heaven to sit on the throne.

Jerusalem said, Elijah what about me? Elijah said, Jerusalem you will have to sanctify in the kingdom in the Children of the women at the appointed time to give you a Son with your Spirit as I promised at the appointed time to give you beautiful children as your Brothers in heaven to populate the earth for thee to live among the children created for thee on the days of salvation in kingdoms from your flesh to be accepted by the ETERNAL.

Jerusalem said this time I will not be ashamed, I will make a Perfect Son with holy seed to populate the earth with perfect Children in my flesh. Elijah said they will be holy Spirits in kingdoms passing on the holy seed from your promised Son by the WORD, they don't need salvation, when they are dead their Spirits will sleep in the earth and wake up on the days of salvation to go above. When the last spirit from the seed of god is purged from your flesh you shall return to earth from heaven to be Queen of the earth with perfect Spirits of creation living in your flesh with Eternal life on earth.

Jerusalem said, O Elijah, all this work to be your righteous Queen, out of all this evil much good will come through our Son by the WORD. Elijah said you will be happy with him and he will have perfect children that will give you much Joy, and not your first god born in sin to face torment and sorrows.

Jerusalem said my Father told me I'll be your Queen before I was kidnapped by devils I am happy to be your Queen.

Zion said, my daughter now you can see how blessed you are; CHRIST created your King Elijah, Lord and Judge of the whole by the WORD to save you and give you perfect children on earth, therefore when the time come to sanctify cleave unto your husband in the body of Noah to be as I was in the body Adam, until you wake from sleep to manifest to have His Son with your spirit by the WORD.

Zion said Jerusalem when I wake from rest I will be with you on earth till the time come to resurrect to see judgment on the devils and godly spirits in Hades. Elijah said the earth is now tilled from the filth from ancient devils and violence, the couples in the vessel are young and healthy Jerusalem when you awake sanctify in the body of an old woman so you don't get hassle for peace. Zion said all I want is to rest in peace while its seed time, I have enough of living in the flesh.

EXORTATION BY ZION

Zion said my daughter when the godly spirits return from Hades they will blame you and want to make war on your children they will enter kingdoms to have control, you will have to fight for your children so demons don't seduce them, they will seduce mankind to kill them to have control in kingdoms, we have seen judgment, our body burnt in fire, we have witnessed judgment on godly spirits in the flood our eyes can see Elijah in the body of Noah, so we can do the same as Spirits to live in any body from our flesh until the appointed time come to see judgment in heaven.

Zion said Jerusalem as long as we are on earth we will continue as a beacon of light until we have living Spirits in the light in our flesh. Jerusalem said if Elijah did not save the couples in the vessel we would have no flesh to inherit on earth Mother, the Testament for Elijah to return spirits of the dead in the flood to devils in Hades and save the couples in the vessel is to make kingdoms for Christ to create Spirits to glory is a good plan to have perfect people on earth when He return on the days of salvation and return the godly spirits that has no faith to devils is righteous.

Elijah said; Jerusalem you are a free Spirit, when you awake you will be like a fugitive upon the earth fleeing from one body to the next to avoid persecution by godly spirits after the return from captivity to warn mankind of fire if they don't have faith, they will seduce mankind and Israelites to blame you for making them to suffer and will want to kill our people on earth to eliminate them as they did to our brothers in heaven and seduce to rape our daughters through jealousy.

Jerusalem said, Elijah do the same to them as you did when I was in Babylon in the flesh and remove them from the earth, she said, Elijah where can I hide if I am still on earth, the demon spirits will see me as they are no more human and want to enter the same body I am in to punish me for making them not perfect?

Elijah said hark to my words when Israel return he will search for you and enter the same body with you and want to do the same as he did to you in Babylon, and want to kill our Son and blame you because he is a godly spirit from the fire because he is not accepted, If he enter the same body you are in to disturb your peace cry to me and I will return to thee, to punish him seven times more than he received from the devils. He will use every opportunity ensnare thee with godly spirits, any godly spirit that enter the same body with Zion or You is strictly forbidden (1Pet5-10: Rev5.1-6)

THE NEW EARTH

The vessel was sailing in the mist over the water, Elijah commanded the wind to come and clear the mist and looked upwards and saw CHRIST on the throne and there was much clapping in heaven. The water of the flood began to recede to its setting in the chasm of the earth day after day, mountain tops began to appear until the water reached its level its level causing the earth to be divided between land and oceans of water, seas and Islands.

The earth was wet and muddy with trees standing with no leaves Elijah commanded the wind to come from the north and blow the water and the mud upon the earth to the south and freeze the water and the mud into Ice and it was so. Elijah commanded the wind to come from the north and blow the water and mud on the earth to the south and freeze it to ice and it was so by the WORD

Elijah commanded the sun to dry the water upon the earth and it was so, He commanded fresh filtered water flow and filtered Water began to flow coming down mountain into streams and rivers to the sea throughout the earth and it was so.

The earth was thoroughly cleansed, the bones of beasts, to the tiniest of creatures and human bones was engraved with fossils in the earth for future generations to explore the history of the flood.

Elijah commanded the wind to come in the south with power and blow on the ice in the north to east to south and circulate south west to north to make mist and clouds to moisturize the earth to make rain for the people to grow food, this was to be the wind system to circulate hot and cold air around the earth to make mist and clouds to shelter the earth from the heat of the sun and for the sun to melt the ice in the oceans until the Passover is complete in kingdoms for Salvation with perfect Spirits of creation on earth without godly spirits in the flesh of Zion and Jerusalem forever by the WORD. To give CHRIST the VICTORY to complete the Passover on earth with Spirits of Christ to be as it was in the beginning with CHRIST and ZION without god and gods in their flesh.

THE VESSEL SAILING IN OCEAN

Mean while the trees that survived the flood began to shoot flowers to bear fruit, the earth began to look green with pasture with everything new. Elijah let out the birds to fly to the earth, the fishes started to follow the vessel schools of dolphin began to jump out of the water. Large whales spouting out water, sharks with their fins above swimming next to the vessel. There was much excitement among the people looking through portholes.

The vessel was sailing silently in the ocean navigated by satellite and by solar Batteries Elijah called for a jet stream and said to Zion you have a choice to go to any part of the earth to rest in peace till you awake Elijah and Jerusalem gave her a hug and kiss and off she went with the wind to find a place she could sleep in peace till she awake from sleep.

When Zion did not return Elijah called for a jet stream for Jerusalem to take her to any place she want to sleep in peace he gave her a hug and kiss and off she went with the wind, She decided to take rest where she once lived her parents when she was young and went to the thermal pool and saw Zion crying.

A VIRTUOUS WIFE IS A CROWN TO HER HUSBAND (PRO12.4: GEN9. 20 IS 54.5)

Jerusalem asked; Mother why are you crying? Zion said I am still on earth and have to wait until the earth is populated to go above.

Jerusalem said Mother don't be sorrowful when we wake from sleep we will see the kingdoms from the couples saved populating the earth. Zion said my daughter I dread having to wake up to be in the body of an old woman before I go to heaven to ask godly spirits to have mercy before mankind and Israelites before I face judgment by angels in the tabernacle. Zion said, Jerusalem you were born on earth for Elijah to be your king and Lord with the WORD, when you wake from sleep you will be the mother of living Spirits through your Son and children from him populating perfect Spirits plus when CHRIST return to earth He will create Spirits to end salvation in Kingdoms forever.

Jerusalem said: Mother I want to sleep and not wake while the couples are passing seed to make kingdoms how can I sanctify? Zion said My daughter, Elijah is your King, sanctified in Noah return to the vessel and sanctify and cling onto his Spirit and you will be as one in Noah till you awake to have the promised Son by the WORD, Zion fell asleep while talking to Jerusalem. She took the jet stream and back to the vessel and waited in the sanctum.

Elijah returned to the sanctum after speaking to the couples and saw Jerusalem and said could you not find a place to sleep? She said Thou art my husband in the body of Noah I want to sanctify and cleave unto thee my King and sleep till I wake up to be in the body of an old woman to give me the Son you promise me by the WORD. Jerusalem sanctified in Noah just as Zion sanctified with CHRIST as male and Female in Adam.

ELIJAH NAVIGATE THE VESSEL TO CRUISE AROUND THE EARTH

Elijah began his journey in the Pacific Ocean coasting the continent putting couples ashore and animals all the way to Australia then from this continent began to do the same coasting the Islands and the continent in the Indian Ocean putting couples ashore and letting out animals and creatures out up to India and Arabia and gave the Testament of Christ in the Ark to the sons of Noah to make copies to pass on to all on earth. Elijah said to all the people he put ashore he moved on be fruitful and populate the earth and tell your children to tell their children in future generations to have Faith for eternal peace for their kingdom to his blessing and it was so.

From Arabian Gulf Elijah began to coast the continent of Africa in the Indian Ocean and put couples ashore and let out animals and creatures, coasting along Africa on the Atlantic and putting couples ashore and animals and creatures, said to all couples he put ashore on the continent of Africa to populate and make kingdoms for Salvation and to have Faith and tell their children to tell their children to have faith to have eternal peace for their kingdom to have His blessing and it was so.

Elijah set sail from the continent of Africa on the journey across the Atlantic to the Americas and put the couples along the coast ashore and said to the couples to populate and make kingdoms for salvation to have his blessing and to have faith, tell their children to tell their children to have eternal peace and it was so.

Elijah set sail to Whykibuli put ashore couples and animals and creatures and told them to be fruitful and populate and make kingdoms for salvation to have his blessing to have eternal peace and to tell their children to tell their children to have faith and it was so.

Elijah set the Vessel on a direct course north, when it disappeared out of sight Elijah went up the mountain to have rest and fell asleep to wake up to do righteous work according to the plan for the final Passover for the Kingdoms upon the earth to end Salvation.

1000 YEARS LATER AFTER THE FLOOD

One thousand years after the flood the earth was populated with mankind making Kingdoms for salvation all over the earth.

The godly spirits from the fall of Babylon and the flood in Hades was released to warn mankind of the chaos in Hades, the godly spirits entered the bodies of mankind and instead of seducing them to do good begin to seduce with all sorts of passion to lead them astray.

Israel entered the body of the ruler name Tidal, the godly spirits called Israel King Tidal, Hadassah entered the body of a woman in Sodom she was queen of Sodom. King Tidal/Israel did the same as he did in Babylon godly spirits seduced spirits in mankind to capture men in the nations and they became slaves to build Sodom for King Tidal and his queen Hadassah, She did the same as in Babylon seduced the woman she entered to be a Whore and corrupted the women that was kidnapped in the nations for prostitution.

The other kings did the same in Gomarrah seduced the men they entered to capture men to be slaves to build palaces and kidnap there women for prostitution. The two cities became the sin cities on the planet with much activity and commerce.

ABRAHAM AND SARAH AND HER MAID HAGAR (2PET2.14)

The Sprits which was not seen is revealed so the reader can know what took place in that generation as humans can't see a spirit. Jerusalem awake from spiritual sleep, she went roaming around the earth, she saw Sarah an old woman the wife of Abraham, and she entered the body of Sarah and cast out Sarah spirit from her flesh and sanctified in Sarah body.

Abraham had no Idea that woman who was his wife was no more, neither could he see any change in Sarah except she had suddenly become frigid and has no desire to have sex him, he accepted this to be old age and was good companion for him. Jerusalem liked baking cakes for him, while Hager did the cooking for them and the herdsmen.

Abraham and his herdsmen went from place to place with his herd of cattle and goats grazing his animals pitching their tent here and there for the night and moving on next day when they got to Sodom with his herd he pitched his tent away from Sodom, cleaned up himself and left Jerusalem and Hager and went to Sodom to have a good time. He met a woman, unknowing to him she was possessed by the godly spirit Hadassah whore of Babylon released from Hades

Abraham began to boast to the woman of his wealth, not knowing he was entertained by a godly spirit in the woman seducing him and he began to respond to the whore of Sodom, Hadassah said: Abraham why a wealthy man like you come to Sodom, if you have a wife? He said my wife is not interested in sex with me she is frigid. Hadassah seduced the spirit in the same body as her to give Abraham a good time. He promised to see her again.

After Abraham left Sodom city, Hadassah went to the palace, She said my king this man Abraham came to Sodom, he is rich he gave me a lot of money I asked him why he came to Sodom to have sex with prostitutes he said his wife is frigid like a Hebrew, he said he worship God to death. You must meet him to take all his wealth from him.

Abraham left Jerusalem in the tent and came to Sodom again looking for the woman that gave him a good time before she saw him and hurriedly went to tell Israel Abraham is back in Sodom, Israel said you know what to do give him a good time and after introduce me to him.

After she gave Abraham a good time, King Tidal came and she introduced Abraham to him, Israel said through the mouth of Tidal I understand you are a man of God in Sodom? Abraham said I worship God to Death. Israel switched came out from the body of Tidal and entered the body of Abraham to take him to his tent see this Hebrew woman as Hadassah told him she killed the last two Hebrews on earth in Babylon.

Abraham entered the tent to his surprise saw Jerusalem in the body of Sarah, as spirits can see each other, (Abraham's spirit was non active) Jerusalem said get out of the body of Abraham, the devils removed your eyes before you came from captivity. Israel said through the mouth of Abraham Now that I have found thee again I will not spear thee for suffering in the fire in Hades with multitudes of godly spirits from the fall of Babylon and the flood.

Israel said: Elijah has released me and multitudes of godly spirits and we can enter any body we want to tempt the spirits in the kingdom to see if they have faith in him. The godly spirits released shall not spear thee for making them not perfect, they blame you for making Elijah cast them from the face of the earth to devouring fire in Hades.

Jerusalem began to cry; Elijah I am in distress. Israel is threatening me, he is angry he said the godly spirits is coming after me for making them to suffer in fire in Hades, Elijah come and save me from these godly spirits, all Israel is talking about is violence to take over the earth with godly spirits as mankind can't see them, he is abusive to me and said the godly spirits will seduce the spirits in their body to lose faith in you and seduce the spirits to make images of them to worship them as there god in the nations on earth.

Jerusalem cried Elijah wake up to send these godly spirits back to Hades. Israel said through the mouth of Abraham I am the king of the spirits and they do as I say and have authority over all spirits with him for the earth, even the spirit in the body of Abraham is from my seed, boasting to Jerusalem Abraham worship me as his God to Death and you are in the body of his woman.

Jerusalem said his woman spirit was in my flesh and I have power to go in and out of any woman in my flesh and cast out there spirit and there is nothing you can do about it and this applies to you if you enter the same body I am in.

Elijah appeared, she said: O Elijah, Israel is abusive he said he and the godly spirits will take over the earth and seduce spirits to lose faith in you to worship them in the nations as there gods. Israel in the body of Abraham fell on the ground, froth coming from his mouth and could not speak.

Elijah commanded: Abraham stand to you feet, and follow me to Sodom to show this Tyrant judgment that he did not see in Babylon, Israel blocked the ears of Abraham so he could not hear what Elijah was saying. Elijah said Israel this is an example of what I will do which you did not see when I removed the devils from the earth if he hurt or threaten Jerusalem while she is on earth.

Elijah said, Israel you and the godly spirits cried in Hades for mercy to release you to return to do good for mankind and to warn them of the fire in Hades with devils and seduce the spirits to have faith in me to have eternal peace so they don't end in fire, instead of seducing the spirits in mankind to do good when returned from captivity you have gone back to your old way doing the same as you did in Babylon with your filth in Sodom and Gomarrah to corrupt mankind in prostitution and slavery to live in fear of you.

Israel said through the mouth of Abraham, because you are the Judge of the earth you want to show your power over sprits on earth and want to destroy Sodom because Hadassah set fire to the body of Zion and Jerusalem in Babylon.

Elijah said there is not one good in Sodom or on earth that is like Jerusalem, if you can bring me a righteous Spirit in Sodom as Jerusalem I will not destroy Sodom, so and find me a righteous Spirit in Sodom.

Israel went and returned and brought Hadassah, Elijah said you bring me your whore from Babylon doing the same in the body of this woman in Sodom as a righteous Spirit, the woman fell and began to froth in the mouth in fear, Elijah commanded the woman to stand and flee from Sodom.

Elijah commanded balls of fire to come from the sky to fall on Sodom and Gomarrah the inhabitants began running here and there; the wind came and began to spread fire all over Sodom and Gomarrah. People began crying, God to Sodom save us. All Israel in the body of Abraham could do is watch the city he built end in fire. Elijah Israel the next time you make Jerusalem cry to me it will be you returning in the fire in Hades.

THE MYSTERY REVEAL HADASSAH SWITCH BODY AND ENTERED HAGER

Hadassah switched and entered the body of Hager, the cook and servant of Abraham to be with Israel in the body of Abraham, Israel said to Elijah I will not touch Jerusalem or hurt her.

THE PROMISE SON

Elijah said to Israel: I promised to give Jerusalem a Son by the WORD with her Spirit She will conceive spiritual seed in the name of Isaac with her holy egg and through Isaac his Sons will pass on the holy seed to populate the earth with righteous Spirits in Kingdoms from her flesh and they will be my people. Israel said what about my people? Elijah said: If they have faith in me and prepare their body for salvation they will have Eternal peace if not they will join you for having no faith according to the promise I made before you took the law.

Elijah said to Israel in the body of Abraham Jerusalem will conceived the holy seed in the name Isaac to populate the earth with holy Spirits in the Light in the flesh of Jerusalem and Zion.

Jerusalem said O Elijah now you have given me your blessed Son in the sight of Israel don't leave me alone with them take me with you, Elijah said: Jerusalem Ill return when you are ready to give birth to my Son with everlasting life. Elijah said to Israel you know what I will do if you touch Jerusalem and my only Son while I am away. Israel said through the mouth of Abraham, I will not put a hand on Jerusalem with your Blessed Son by the WORD. Israel said through the mouth of Abraham he will give Hager a son. Elijah said as long as you know Isaac is not your heir. What is born between Hager and Abraham shall be his heir passing on your seed.

Elijah said to Israel look above and see the multitudes of stars, can you count them and tell me how many you see? Israel Said no. Elijah said so shall the seed of Isaac populate the earth with righteous Spirits to go above from your mothers flesh. The spirits from your seed you shall inherit after they are separated from the flesh of Jerusalem if they don't have faith like you after CHRIST cast them out on the days of salvation in kingdoms. Jerusalem is a blessed Spirit and I have give her a blessed SON with the holy seed by the WORD and she will be mother of Kings in her flesh that don't need salvation.

Israel got angry, said so you accept Isaac as your Son and not me? Elijah said Jerusalem is my wife and she is pregnant with holy seed in the name of Isaac by the WORD, if you had faith you would have eternal peace. And your body would be for salvation to create a Blessed Son by the WORD this was your Choice but you put your hope with Satan, so why cry to me now if Jerusalem have a perfect Son to populate on earth you are a jealous god.

GOD-ISRAEL WAS JEALOUS OF ISAAC

Jerusalem Spirit was in the body of Sarah and she gave birth to Isaac, Abraham said: I have not had sex with thee who son is he? I am not his father? Jerusalem said I asked the Lord to give me a Son and I conceived, Isaac is his name. This conception is immaculate Abraham said to have a son in your old age, who is this Lord? Jerusalem said his name is Elijah.

Many years later Israel seduced Abraham to go the mountain to worship his God, and he brought Isaac with him, when he got to the mountain he built an altar put wood on the altar Israel seduced Abraham to tie Isaac to the wood and set the wood on fire as an offering,as he was about to set the wood on fire to burn the body of Isaac on fire. Elijah said Abraham in a firm voice, don't set the wood on fire Isaac is my Son, there is a goat in the bush take it and sacrifice to your God

Israel was afraid Elijah would say the WORD flees from the body of Abraham. Elijah said Abraham I am the Lord, because you have obeyed my voice you shall have a son with Hager to populate from your seed till salvation end. Israel and Hadassah fled from the tent of Abraham and joined the godly spirits in the nations to plan for war for the earth.

Jerusalem saw Isaac was well looked after by Abraham and fell asleep. Abraham and Isaac went everywhere together like a father looking after a Son Isaac met Rebecca and they had many children, Abraham died and had Eternal Peace.

Isaac separated his people from the Israelites and began to populate his people with knowledge of the higher science, the people of Isaac were beautiful and reserved and would not mix, was called Hebrews, by Israel and his Israelites this brought much hatred and constant conflict in that generation

Elijah appeared to Isaac said: My Son I have come to show you a land where you shall dwell and multiply in peace. Elijah took Isaac on a trip around the earth and stopped on an Island separated from the continent.

Elijah said from this Island children from your seed shall multiply and populate in many nations on earth. Elijah explained the plan to put order on earth and the Testament of CHRIST and salvation for kingdoms from his mother's flesh for who are not his people to be for creation. Elijah made a circle and took stones and placed them around the circle and placed stones upon the stones around the circle. And said this is a land mark for when you return on this island for all your children to populate in every nation on earth.

Elijah said: Isaac when you return you shall build a vessel to bring my people on this island with all their livestock to be united in the Kingdom with Spirits in the Light away from those who hate thee on earth.

Isaac built the vessel to plan and all his people took their belongings and livestock on the vessel to sail to the island of light. The rulers seduced by godly spirits in the nation came after Isaac and his children. Elijah commanded stones to fall upon the pursuers and they backed off

A tempest came, the sea became stormy where the vessel was built and a wave, lifted the vessel and brought it to sea and it was on course to the land of milk and honey the people gave Elijah Praise for his greatness Isaac said my father has brought you this island to populate and to go on the continent and multiply his people, Kings shall come out of thee to rule on this island to be united in the kingdom with people of our father to live in peace. Isaac lived to see his people populate on the island to establish themselves and started to go on the continent to populate he fell asleep.

HUNDRED OF YEARS LATER

Many have tried to set order to the issue of heredity which concern them, and want to know how they are connected with the errors of the devils in the beginning and what they have to do for eternal peace in accordance with the testimony of CHRIST to make the covenant the ETERNAL had with the devils while they were in Heaven became obsolete, so all who live on earth can be righteous to live in peace and harmony after Salvation end on earth.

It seem good to me having perfect understanding of the things that went wrong in the beginning to write and put heredity in order so the reader may know the way to eternal life is for people of Elijah and Jerusalem and for those who are not the people of Jerusalem and Elijah must have faith in Elijah to save them to have eternal peace for their body to be created to continue with a righteous Spirit to be accepted by the Eternal created through CHRIST so all on earth be righteous Spirits in the Kingdom to be as it was in the beginning by the WORD with CHRIST and ZION and no godlyspirits of devils in their flesh.

THE TWO SPIRITS ZION AND JERUSALEM

According to the plan to begin the process of judgment on godly spirits, Zion awake from sleep in that generation and sanctified in the body of an old woman in the name of Elizabeth and cast out Elizabeth's spirit to have eternal rest.

Jerusalem awake from sleep and sanctified in the body of a woman called Mary and cast out Mary's spirit and her spirit had eternal rest.

The godly spirits were released after 1000 years in captivity in Hades and were told not to harm Zion and Jerusalem but could entered the body of mankind and tempt them to see if they had faith in Elijah who saved their forefathers in the vessel, but instead they seduced the spirits of mankind to make images of godly spirits in their body and mankind began to carve gods in wood, gold, silver, bronze, stone and worshiping these carvings as there god. The godly spirits seduced the spirits of mankind with their lust to commit every kind of immorality to lose faith and seduced them in their body to worship them as there god in the nation to confuse mankind with false worship in religion to lose faith in Elijah.

The godly spirit Israel entered the body of Mary Jerusalem had sanctified after she woke up from sleep. The godly spirit of god/Cain entered the body of Elizabeth Zion sanctified when she woke from sleep.

Jerusalem began to cry, Elijah I am in the body of Mary, Israel has entered and he is threatening me he said he will make me suffer because you sent him to Hades, he is angry with me for making him not perfect and Jealous of Isaac. Elijah I am afraid it is stressful to be in the same body with Israel he is malicious and base, he has no respect he said I cannot hide from him and all godly spirits released with him from captivity will destroy kingdoms from my flesh until I have no flesh left for salvation. Elijah come and save me from this boaster.

Zion began to cry: Elijah save me from the godly spirit of Cain, he is pestering me and blaming me for being born to suffer in devouring fire, He is jealous of you Elijah because my Father Created you in his kingdom for salvation after the Satan strangled him. Elijah come and save me from god/ Cain, he is in the same body I am in he said Israel has passed on his seed to make Israelites and mankind he said all spirits from his seed is his inheritance on earth to return to Death, I told him if he did not rape my daughter he would not have godly spirits to return to Death. Elijah I am in the body of Elizabeth come and cast him out from this body.

CHRIST ON THE THRONE IN HEAVEN

Jesus was showing Elijah the cities he was construction on one of the planets for the Spirits of the earth, one of his brothers came and said Father said both you must report to him immediately. When they arrived in the tabernacle CHRIST said the godly spirits of Cain and Israel has entered the same body as Zion and Jerusalem and they are making them cry, it is forbidden for godly spirits to enter the same body with Holy Spirits Zion and Jerusalem

CHRIST said: Jesus you are always with me in heaven you will have to return to earth with Elijah, Jerusalem is in the body of a woman called Mary, when you get to earth enter and cast out Israel and sanctify to be an image of yourself in the flesh so you can be seen by humans to confirm the Testament in the ark and to the generation of the Children of the people save in the vessel to have faith in Elijah to rest in eternal peace and to prepare their kingdom for salvation for when I return earth to create Spirits in Kingdoms to continue on earth in righteousness to live the Everlasting Life.

CHRIST said Elijah my Son you have not tasted death in the body to be a Spirit without Flesh after you are dead to minister the WORD. Elijah you will save Zion and Jerusalem and return them to me after you judge them before mankind, Israelites and your people in this generation before multitudes of godly spirits, Elijah, you and Jesus will be the witnesses for Zion and Jerusalem.

CHRIST said Jesus you will use this mission to preach about the kingdom to the spirits of gods in the kingdom to have Faith before I return for their spirits to rest in peace and tell their children the choice they have for peace and salvation of their body to have a Spirit of creation to continue in their image when I return to earth, tell Zion and Jerusalem to have a little patience for their resurrection, after you have finished your mission confirming the Testament of what I will do when I return to earth to Create Spirit in the kingdom to live on earth and to end Salvation forever.

CHRIST said Jesus you have not lived among godly spirits other than god /Cain, multitudes of godly spirits will come against you for telling mankind and Israelites the truth about God and what he did to you sister he called Babylon, tell the gods the doctrine they are following is false and if they continue with this doctrine it will lead them to Death. CHRIST said; Jesus the godly spirits will do everything to remove you from the earth to hide the truth

CHRIST said Elijah you will go in the nations to tell the godly spirits in the body of mankind to repent when you gather them in one place, release Satan from Hades to be with the godly sprits and ask them to repent for making gods to pass on the seed of Death in the flesh of Zion and Jerusalem, Elijah focus on godly spirits in mankind to repent until Jesus bring Zion and Jerusalem to confront them for rape to make gods.

Elijah you and Jesus will be witnesses for Zion and Jerusalem standing before Satan and godly spirit in the body of mankind. CHRIST said: Jesus you have a to complete this mission in 1260 days to prophesy what I will do when I return to earth on the days of salvation to remove spirits of gods from the kingdoms from the flesh of Zion and Jerusalem, while you are prophesying both of you have power to return Satan to Hades and to confirm testimony of flesh and blood on the wood before the Israelites before the flood by Elijah.

THE TWO WITNESSES (REV11.4

Elijah with the word and Jesus was sent by CHRIST on a mission to earth to confirm the Testament of Christ in the ark in the tabernacle in heaven to all on earth, and to be the witnesses to Zion and Jerusalem to begin the process of Judgment on the unholy spirits who has no faith and anti CHRIST to end the suffering of spirits born to Death.

Elijah entered the body of Elizabeth/ Zion was in, godly spirit (Cain) was in fear and asked who are you? Elijah said I am the Holy Spirit created to take your kingdom available for Salvation. Zion said O Elijah He is pestering me cast him out this body im in, Elijah said you either get out in peace or I send you back to Hades, in great fear he went out and entered the body of Judas. Elijah sanctified and manifest and was in his image in flesh to be seen by humans and began to preach repent to the godly spirits in the nations.

Jerusalem was in the body of Mary Jesus entered, Israel said who are you? Are you the CHRIST whose body I hanged on the tree? Jerusalem cried cast him out. Jesus said I command you to get out of this body now or you return to Hades, in great fear he got out and entered the body of Simon Peter.

Jesus sanctified and manifest in his image to be seen by humans in the flesh to begin his mission to tell mankind the truth, to have faith, for peace and to prepare their body for salvation before CHRIST return to earth to create Spirits in Kingdoms with Eternal life.

Jerusalem went in haste to Zion and said Mother Jesus cast out Israel from pestering me and he departed to begin his mission on earth. Zion said my daughter Elijah is back with us and he cast out Cain from this body I am relieved from all his insults making me sorrowful. Zion said now you shall see action by Elijah before godly spirits that returned from captivity and see judgment on Satan in Hades.

Cain in the body of Judas went with godly spirits to Zion with hate, asked, where is the Holy Spirit that cast me out of the body you are in? I understand he brought up Israel while I was in Hades so he had mercy on him and can do the same and have mercy on godly spirits released from captivity we are afraid to return to devils in Hades. A godly spirit said if you and Jerusalem don't ask for mercy Elijah will end our time on earth and return in the fire in Hades.

Zion said he left after he manifest in flesh, the godly spirits asked what is his name, Zion said Elijah, the godly spirits said so he has come to recue you and Jerusalem from us?

The godly spirits went in haste to Jerusalem and saw Jesus with her, Israel in the body of peter said now I have seen CHRIST I shall depart before Elijah come after us to speak the WORD, Israel said I can see you are a Holy Spirit manifest in the flesh if you mention the truth about me and the Sabbath in Babylon, Multitudes of godly spirits will come and remove you from the earth, Jesus looked at him and kept his cool and he left Jerusalem and Jesus he was angry and kept away.

Jesus and Elijah separated themselves to do the work according to the Testament of CHRIST in the ark in the tabernacle in heaven for righteous justice on all godly spirits in the kingdom to have the choice to have eternal peace or return to Death. Elijah began his mission among local people telling them they must have faith like there forefathers to rest in peace, the sinners among you must have mercy, repent for the sins, you that are in the kingdom, I baptize these with water but when CHRIST come they will be will baptized in fire if they don't have faith, repent, repent you having no mercy on the spirits in the kingdom you seduce them to sin, have mercy. Repent.

The godly spirits thought if they repented they would not return to Hades, they seduced the spirits to call Elijah John so mankind would not know Elijah is the Judge over all spirits. This repentance excited the godly spirits thinking there is hope for them not to return to Hades and seduced the spirits to follow Elijah they called John the Baptist, Elijah concentrated to tell the multitudes that followed him the way to new life is salvation and preparation of a clean body, He used Baptism by water as an example for all mankind to have faith in Him for there Kingdom to be created by CHRIST to be accepted as righteous Spirits in the Kingdom in the time of salvation.

Mean while Jesus began to preach in temples and synagogues about Salvation, and said there kingdom is for creation and they are spirits of gods and whoever has faith will have eternal peace, there was much debate by the Jews, they asked, Jesus where did you get this doctrine of salvation and eternal peace we live by the Law of God our father and there is nothing in the law that say we must have faith to have eternal peace, we worship God our father to save us and not the flesh of our mother.

Jesus said I know you are from the seed of God your father and the promise that was made to him before he took the oath to live by the law to Death that he would receive every spirit that has no faith like him in the gate when salvation begin and that all kingdoms from the flesh of Jerusalem on earth is her inheritance for my Father to create Spirits in kingdoms. This promise was made to God your father before he took the Law to be a prophet to the gods. He had no Faith to rest in eternal peace. This doctrine was not know the Jews they became hostile to Jesus, this was not written to know they need salvation, some shouted this is a mystery, others shouted he is talking in parables he is seduced by Belzebob, Jesus walked away, He told them the truth no point ageing.

Jesus went to another temple and everyone wanted to hear about this new doctrine: He said, I came not to abolish the law of Judah but to tell the truth so the Kingdom will be brought to perfection, for as you know all of you in the kingdom are not perfect. When the kingdom is fully established on earth the law of Judah will be obsolete so all Spirits created in the kingdom will live by the Testament by my father in Heaven.

You have been told by your forefathers that ws saved in the flood to teach their children to have faith in the Lord to have eternal peace, don't be angry with me because I tell you the truth, you are better than the Pharisee who want you to observe the law, for he had no faith and was condemned for what he did with the ancients to be a king.

You have heard the gods say an eye for an eye and a tooth for a tooth. But I say if any one strike you turn the other cheek so you are not tempted to do lose faith to fall for doing the same as the godly spirits who do not care in there kingdom.

If you are not perfect, and you love who made you that way there is no gain and you will do the same as the pagans, you must be perfect to be in heaven as my Father who is not God your father who knows what he did and the reason why you are not perfect, so while you are in the kingdom have faith to save yourself.

Jesus said: when you fast dont be like those hypocrites that are in the kingdom they are condemned godly spirits leading you astray on earth, have faith and prepare your selves for salvation for your Kingdom to be created with a Spirit by my father in heaven to be where there are no devils and thieves. You cannot serve two masters, you will either hate the one who made you not perfect of love the one who can give you eternal peace for the Spirit Created perfect in to have everlasting life, do not be anxious about tomorrow, today's trouble is enough for you to handle as you do not know if you will live tomorrow

Jesus went on to say the way to Death is for many who has no faith and only those who has faith will have eternal peace for their kingdom to be created to populate the earth with perfect spirits. Not every one of you in the kingdom who call me lord shall enter heaven. Only through salvation of a kingdom with as spirit that has faith a Spirit will be created perfect.

Jesus told the Jews in the temple don't be afraid of the chief Phrarises everything that he has hidden shall be told so you can know the truth and what I have said to you don't keep it as a secrete tell it to everyone, do not be afraid who can kill your body and can't kill the spirit. The Pharisy is in fear of Elijah who will cast his godly spirit in hell. Don't imagine I came bring peace on earth to godly spirits but to tell you the way to Everlasting life and the way to establish the Kingdoms on earth through the King with the WORD with my Father from the flesh of Zion to remove your enemies from the earth.

Jesus sais to the Jews there is none greater than Elijah in the Kingdom, The scripture speaks about Him and what he did and why he destroyed Sodom, and none of you comprehend to this day was to make an example to Israel if he ever touch his Son Isaac what he will do, his children live among you who you call Hebrews. Jesus said learn from me and you shall rest in peace and your kingdom shall have a Spirit in the Light with Eternal life.

Jesus said when a godly spirit has gone out of a body it enters in another body and settle there and seduce the spirit of the man not to have faith like him and to be wicked like him. Jesus came to an end of his discourse and the people were amazed at his teaching for he taught with authority.

Jesus went in a temple made of wood and stone, he started to preach to mankind, he told them they must have faith and must prepare their body for salvation to have eternal peace so when my Father come to earth on the days of Salvation he can create a Spirit your kingdom to live the everlasting life, the people asked, Jesus if your Father is a creator tell Him to give us a sign and we will believe our body can be created with a new Spirit to be perfect.

The godly spirits spoke to Jesus through the mouth of mankind, Jesus said to the godly spirits in the body of mankind you are a bunch of Hippocrets no sign will be given. And walked away Jesus mission is to tell the truth that is hidden and the way of life in the kingdom and salvation and the testament of CHRIST what He will do on the days of salvation. He had no time for argument. Jesus returned to Zion and Jerusalem and her people through Isaac they are called Hebrews, the Hebrews asked Jesus many questions, He said there home is in heaven, many homes is built for them when they leave the earth, we must forgive those who are against us in the kingdom, they have godly spirits in their body that lead many astray through temptation so you will not have faith for eternal peace, he told his people his mission is to tell the spirits born in sin they have a choice to have faith and to prepare their body for Salvation so all on earth will be of creation without sinners.

Jesus told the Hebrews you are righteous Spirits and you must be happy and not cry and comfort each other and show mercy and love as they are children of Elijah and when they die there Spirit will be in Heaven when their time come for resurrection, he told them they are the people of the earth and there Spirit is in the Light and when they die they will see how beautiful they are in the light among angels in heaven.

ISRAEL IN THE BODY OF SIMON PETER
(HOS.9.7-8:4.1-16)

Israel sent godly spirits in the body of Jews to expose John before multitudes he Baptized in the Jordan, the Jews have no Idea what is going on in their body. The godly spirits Know John is Elijah they can see him just as Elijah can see them in the body of Jews.

A godly spirit spoke through the mouth of a Jew: John are you the CHRIST? John said no, another asked, are you Elijah? He said I Baptize those who has faith in the water to prepare the way for when CHRIST come in the kingdom to return to him who sent you to come and ask me who I am.

Elijah could see many godly spirits that fell in the fall of Babylon that were released from captivity in the body of mankind he said you sinners repent who warned you of the wrath that is at hand I am Baptizing your children who has faith. Repent for making them to be born in sin. The WORD is ready to root out spirits from your seed in the Kingdom for the earth to be free from sinners, repent, Mankind had no Idea of this spiritual confrontation taking place as the godly spirits were using their eyes and blocking their ears

Satan was released from captivity and was among the godly spirits by the Jordan river in the body of mankind. Elijah said the time has come for all godly spirits in the Kingdom in the flesh of Zion and Jerusalem to repent for your sins.

A godly spirit asked through the mouth of a human, are you Elijah? Elijah said I am with the WORD and was sent to bear witness to Zion and Jerusalem you held in captivity

Another godly spirit asked are you the CHRIST, Elijah said I am the One who heard your father crying in the bush in the wilderness and brought him up on milk and honey and he is among you.

Satan and the godly spirits were afraid of Elijah with the WORD through experience of judgment and kept quiet. Elijah said he who was with the king of devils repent, he who made Israelites with his mother Repent, he who made mankind not perfect repent, he who raped to make a god like him Repent, he who came to earth to rape and make a god to be a sinner and murderer Repent there was silence.

Jesus brought Zion and Jerusalem to the river Jordan and they stood next to Elijah, Elijah said repent, there was silence. Zion looked at Satan, god/Cain, Israel and the multitudes of godly spirits and said, the day of judgment has come, the spirits in there humanity cannot see this spiritual confrontation. Satan and the godly spirits was In fear thinking Jesus is the CHRIST with Elijah on earth to do battle to send them in the fire with Death.

Zion said today judgment will come on the sinner who raped me to make a godly spirit in my flesh, he is among you godly spirits standing in my flesh, Zion said Satan come forth so the gods can see you for the godly spirits in there humanity can see the sinner who made gods all over the earth to know why they are born in sin from your corrupt seed from Death.

Zion said Satan don't be afraid, come forth and repent before all these godly spirits, Satan began to tremble the Spirit of the Sun is shining bright to pull him up from the earthy Satan fell on the ground like a epileptic shaking on the ground speechless in Fear thinking Jesus was the CHRIST of the ETERNAL with Elijah who removed him and the other devils from the earth to Hades for raping holy women. The Spirit of the Sun waiting to pulled up Satan from the earth back to Hades

Zion said, all spirits who can hear today before Judgment begin, I asked Satan to repent for raping me before Elijah and Jesus who can see my adversary, I am asking all you godly spirits to have mercy on me for making a god to be born in sin from the seed Satan of Death.

Zion said; Elijah is the judge standing next to me, he who want to make war for the earth come and stand next to me, Elijah has released you from captivity in Hades, you raped my daughter to make a god to be wicked like you come forward and repent before all these godly spirits released with you, he began to cry through the mouth of Judas I repent for this rape to make a god like me, have mercy I don't want to return to Hades, Zion said let it be known to spirits all over the earth you had no faith to have eternal peace and rape my daughter to make a god for the devils.

Zion said to all the godly spirits let it be known to the last generation of spirits from your seed I came to the river Jordan and stood before Satan and a multitude of spirits to witness I asked Satan to repent for raping me to make a god/Cain and he had no mercy before the judge of the whole earth.

Zion looked up and said: Holy Eternal Father it is a sin to make a god on earth I asked Satan to repent and ask god (Cain) to forgive me for making him born in sin, they had no faith to have eternal peace and did the same as Satan and rape my daughter who is a witness before all these sprits in the kingdom. Elijah picked up Zion in the body of Elizabeth in his arms and walked to the pool in the river Jordan and dipped her in the pool of water and told her she committed no sin in the Spirit and they returned to join Jerusalem and Jesus as witnesses.

Jerusalem in the body of Mary stood between Jesus Zion and Elijah she looked at the multitudes of godly spirits in the kingdom and Satan, She said Satan you kidnapped me to make gods come and stand before the judge of the earth and repent for making gods to be born in sin. Satan come forward and boast to the godly spirits in kingdoms in my flesh how much power you have on earth for spirits to live by your law to Death.

Jerusalem said: I speak clearly before the godly spirits in the kingdom and command you Satan to come and repent before the judge of the whole earth for keeping me in captivity to make gods and to ask the gods to have mercy on me for making them to be born in sin.

Satan fell on the ground with an attack of epilepsy froth coming out of his mouth trembled, afraid of Elijah and thinking Jesus is the CHRIST the ETERNAL created to send all devils back to Death in the everlasting fire. The Sun pulled up Satan from the earth and the tempest came and took him away to fall in the mouth of the waters to Hades to await final judgment.

Jerusalem commanded Israel to come forward and boast before the judge of the whole earth you are a mighty God who created the world before Zion and CHRIST who can see his enemy who hanged his body on a tree. Israel was afraid to come forward thinking Jesus is the CHRIST who cast him out of the body of Mary and entered the body of Simon peter.

Jerusalem said you kept me in captivity to make Israelites come and repent before the judge of the earth. Tell the godly spirits gathered here how cruel you were to me to live by the law till you were dead. Repent for killing all my brothers and hanging the body of my Father on a tree for all Israelites to know the truth why you are not perfect and did not have faith in the judge to have eternal peace and why you were sent to Hades. Tell them why you wanted to kill Isaac my blessed Son by the WORD when you returned from captivity. Jerusalem commanded Israel, repent before all your godly spirits who want to make war for the earth.

Israel cried through the mouth of Peter have mercy on me, I don't want to return to Hades, I will tell all Israelites to have faith in Elijah to have eternal peace for salvation to prepare their kingdom for creation. Jerusalem said tell them to forgive me for making them not perfect so all Israelites on earth to know you repented and ask them to forgive me. Israel was in fear of returning in captivity said I repent.

Jerusalem commanded god /Cain to come forward to repent for rape to make a god who is as wicked like you and slaying the body of all my brothers from the earth. Because of you all mankind and Israelites are born not perfect passing on your accursed seed to make spirits for Satan to live by the law to Death. If you had faith in Elijah you would have eternal peace but did the same as you father to rape an commit murder spilling the blood of holy Son of my Father. Elijah is a witness. Because of your sin sprits are populating the earth with your wickedness making kingdoms for salvation. Your sin brought no joy to me but much sorrow to spirits that is released from Hades.

Come forward and repent before Me Jesus Zion and Elijah for your sin and ask all Israelites and mankind for mercy for being born in sin, because you rape me they are not perfect populating on earth passing on the seed of Death with disease in my flesh all over the earth. Repent and ask the spirits to have mercy on me for being born in sin and to prepare their kingdom for salvation to have eternal peace.

Elijah picked up Jerusalem in the body of Mary and Jesus Picked up Zion and they walked to the pool Elijah dipped Jerusalem in the pool and said your Spirit did not sin it's a sin to make a god in your flesh to face Death in the fire. There was lightning and sparks on the water followed by thunder and rain. The multitude of godly spirits that was gathered by the Jordan for this spiritual show down before the battle for the earth begin The godly spirits seduced the spirits in there humanity to ran away in fear of the Elijah saying WORD.

JESUS, ZION, JERUSALEM WENT WITH ELIJAH WHERE HE WAS STAYING

Elijah said: Jesus these godly spirits will come after you to stop you from telling mankind the truth about Salvation and the way to eternal life is through Christ creating Spirits to be righteous in the flesh of Zion and Jerusalem and want their spirits to lose faith to battle with them for the earth, they will do everything to make sure CHRIST is not known and make the spirits in there humanity believe you are the Christ to populate spirits for battle and to stop you from finishing your mission therefore I will pass on the WORD to you to finish Testifying what our Father will do when he come in the time of Salvation and to protect Zion and Jerusalem and our people.

In the meantime I will take my rest and when you are finished with your mission Pass on the Word to me so I can carry on with the work I am created to do, when you Zion and Jerusalem are in heaven you will see the final Judgment on devils in Hades and godly spirits released in this generation. It is important you finish you mission so judgment on the spirits is justified to end Salvation 0f Kingdoms in the flesh of Zion and Jerusalem for all Spirits on earth to be CHRIST in the kingdom to be justified to live in peace and harmony to enjoy the prosperity in the worlds above.

Elijah said I will tell those I have baptized to follow you to learn more about salvation and their choice for eternal peace.

JESUS SHOW HIS POWER OVER GODLY SPIRITS

Jesus entered a synagogue preach the good news for spirits in there humanity in the kingdom to have faith, and the way to eternal life and salvation of kingdoms a man possessed with a godly spirit cried out what business have you with us Jesus? Have you come to destroy us? I know who you are you are a holy One. Jesus said hold your tongue and come out of this man.

The godly spirit convulsed and gave a loud cry and came out of the man. All in the synagogue were amazed. Saying to each other what is this? Now Jesus is showing us he has power over demons doing what the chief Pharisee cannot do commanded the godly spirit to come out and they obey him. From that moment his fame spread everywhere.

A man came to his house said Jesus a demon is making my wife sick come and tell it to go away, Jesus came entered the house when the demon saw Jesus it screamed through the woman's mouth, Jesus said get out of her and don't return Jesus said give her something to eat.

That day many who were sick and possessed with godly spirits were queuing up to outside his door, he cured many suffering from all kind of disease from Death and commanded the godly spirits to come out from them.

A godly spirit said to Israel in the body of Peter everyone is looking for Jesus to cast us out tell him to go elsewhere he said to Jesus the people are complaining; Jesus said this is one of the reasons I an sent to cast you out from the same body Jerusalem is in and to cast out godly spirits so spirits in there humanity can know the truth you are hiding from them to lead them astray and not to have faith for eternal peace.

A leper came and fell at the feet of Jesus crying, Jesus he said: Heal me from this disease from Death, Jesus said do you have faith it can be done for you? yes he said only you Jesus have the power to make me clean. Jesus said if that is your wish go and wash yourself in the pool and you will be clean from this disease from Death. And the leprosy left his body immediately.

With the result of healing and casting out demons from the people, he could not walk freely as multitudes came for him to heal them, so he went to the open field and told them the power of the

WORD and they must have faith in Elijah to save them as there fore fathers in the flood and to tell their children to have faith in the only savior to rest in peace as salvation is far off.

They brought a paralytic forward in the crowd and said Jesus he has a demon command the demon to get out of him, the demon began to cry through the man's mouth, the crowd shouted go away from him, Jesus said you heard the crowd get out and told the paralyzed to get up and walk. The crowd said we give you Praise Jesus with the power of the WORD demons cry when you speak.

The Pharisee said Jesus why are you always among the sick, Jesus said you are not righteous and can't heal the people afflicted with disease and possessed by godly spirits. The Pharisee said they are complaining about you saying you make them cry and cast out spirit like Elijah who sent them to Hades.

Jesus said they cry because the time is at hand for spirits in there humanity to know the truth about what is happening in their body, they are being led astray by false worship and a doctrine that is false so they don't know about CHRIST and Elijah their savior and the choice the they have for eternal peace like their forefathers, the sin of mankind is forgiven but who is against Elijah and have no faith in him will face Death, I hope the spirit in the body you are in can hear and his eyes can see so he don't fall like you.

Jesus took a few followers with him across the sea to get away from the crowd, and suddenly there was a storm, Jesus pretended to be asleep and the godly spirits in the body of his followers was afraid, Jesus could see them just as they could see him and thought it was a trap Jesus would send them back to Hades in the tempest if they tried to get out the body of his followers cried Jesus show us your power and stop the tempest.

Jesus commanded the wind to stop and said you godly spirits are cowards and have no faith and was afraid I was going to send you back to Hades, they said we can't fight you even the wind obey you.

When they got ashore they went to a cemetery and there was a man chained to a sepulcher when the godly spirit saw Jesus it began to cry loudly through the man's mouth Jesus what business is it of yours to be in this grave yard go away, Jesus said get out of the body of this man right now or you shall return to Hades an in fear of returning to the fire in Hades got out, Jesus told his followers to unchain the man you can return to your home in peace.

Jesus entered a synagogue a rabbi said Jesus my daughter is dead could you bring her back to life, Jesus said don't be afraid to have faith go to your home she is alive and give her something to eat. The Pharisee said: Jesus why the people who follow you don't wash their hands when they eat? Jesus replied, listen to me all of you godly spirits in the body of Jews in this synagogue you seduce their spirits in there humanity to fornicate to do double dealing and be jealous of Hebrews who are holy people, you want to do your wickedness to them while you are in the body of Jew, you are unclean spirits, a Jew fell at his feet he was death and dumb, Jesus put his finger in the man's ear to un block his ear and said I commanded you godly spirit to loosen his tongue and get out. The Jew heard what Jesus said and began to speak. Jesus told him to have Faith so you don't perish.

The Pharisee was angry and said through the mouth of a Jew can you give us proof CHRIST is on the throne in heaven, Jesus said you want all Jews to worship you as the almighty God in this generation so they don't know what you did to the body of CHRIST to be a prophet to teach gods to live by the law. The reason they worship you is because they are of your seed and not like Isaac of creation.

Jesus said to him in the body of Peter stop following me, you put you hope in Satan when you took the law and blaspheme CHRIST and Elijah, If you want to follow me tell the Jews in this generation the Truth of what you have done and follow me to the cross if you have faith, what advantage if the Jews follow you and have no faith like you in salvation when there kingdom could be for creation with Spirits Like Isaac to be in heaven. They will blame you for making them not perfect to suffer, I am ashamed what you did to be in the same body of Jerusalem, My father will punish you when the time come for what you and god you father did.

Jesus told Israel in the body of peter, I will tell you what is going to happen to you before it takes place. Elijah has tasted death and is a Spirit and will deal with every one of you with Spiritual judgment and it will be justified and walked outside.

THE GODLY SPIRITS HAVE A COUNCIL MEETING

A godly spirit said in the meeting the godly spirits in my area are complaining Jesus is casting out there spirit from the body they possess and make them cry and tremble when they have no flesh on their spirit. Chief what can you do? We are more in fear of Jesus than Elijah. The spirits are in fear they will return to Hades to be with devils.

Another godly spirit said Elijah was preaching to the spirits in there humanity to have faith like there forefathers he saved in the vessel and warning us to repent, now all his followers are following Jesus, sooner or later the spirits in there humanity will have faith in Jesus to have eternal peace will stop following the Law and we will lose control in the kingdom to seduce the spirits to fuck to lose faith in you, if you want to be the God of the spirits on earth.

Another godly spirit said Chief: Elijah said he was a witness to Zion and Jerusalem we know in Babylon but we don't know Jesus where he came from, we know he is not a god as no gods have power to heal the sick from the disease from Death. Jesus preach to the spirits in there humanity when his Father return to earth is to kick our ass from the kingdoms from the flesh of Zion and Jerusalem to make every Spirit in their Flesh Perfect for our spirits he cast out who has no faith face Judgment by Elijah and The Spirit of the Sun to face Death.

Another godly spirit said chief the spirits in there humanity are gaining confidence when we seduce them or hurt them to feel pain to pray to you as there almighty God instead they say in Jesus name go away and we have to be quiet even the name of Jesus make us fear punishment by devils if we return to Hades. Chief what can you do to regain control in the Kingdom we looked in the scripture, and nothing is mention of CHRIST or ELIJAH or JESUS having Power over godly spirits.

Another godly spirit said chief if the spirits in there humanity put their life in the hand of Elijah we have no chance to seduce them they will stop worshiping you as there God as you can't help them when they pray to you for help, the only way chief is to crucify Jesus and let him die for his followers who don't believe in God so he can return to heaven and we will fight against Elijah for you to be the King of the Earth.

The godly spirit /Cain in the body of Judas said, I stoned the body of Jesus when he was Abel in the beginning I will not have him to be king to rule on earth, I am the first god born on earth, I am father of all of you born from the seed Israel he passed on my seed to you I am the unknown god and I took a lot of heat for all you Jews and Israelites, I am your god and should be the king of the Jews.

Israel said: but it is through my abomination and lust, I have populated Israelites and Jews on earth from your seed, the earth is populated with their spirits in kingdoms, It is through me they are born I should be king of the earth, an Israelite godly spirit said: yes God father we were kings in Babylon and want to be kings over the spirits from our seed and we will fight with you for the earth until there is no flesh left of our mother, the Israelite godly king said god father the sprits in there humanity don't know you, you are the unknown god, it is we who populated the earth while you were in Hades for rape and murder.

Israel in the body of Peter said; I hate Elijah for having power over us, It is I should be his heir instead chose Isaac because Isaac is a Holy Spirit like Him in the light and has repopulated the earth with Hebrews, Jerusalem had Jesus to come and cast me out from the same body as her, she and Zion don't want to mix with us and made us look like filth to repent for our sins in their flesh.

Israel said to god (Cain) in the body of Judas, my godly father Elijah took your kingdom after Satan strangled you, and you want to be king of the spirits on earth, consider how I outsmart the devils to be King of all nations while you were in Hades for two sins for rape and murder.

Israel said I had to hang the body of Adam who hated you for being born in sin, I Killed 144000 Hebrews and made my mother you rape to be my Queen while you were in Hades. I sinned more than the hairs on head of Judas, you think you have the skill to fight against Elijah who removed the devils from the earth while you were in Hades. Can you fight against Jesus who is terrorizing our spirits to get out from kingdoms from the flesh of Jerusalem?

Prove to us godly spirits in this council meeting you hate Jesus and make him return to heaven where he came from and capture Elijah and you will be king of the spirits of gods on the whole earth.

Through the mouth of Judas god/Cain said if I Capture Elijah I will be king in the Kingdom. Israel said you have lust for Jerusalem she will be your queen as well, I have Hadassah as my queen in the body of Magdalene, and here is 30 pieces of silver to feed Judas.

THE godly spirit (Cain) is a jealous god with much hate seeing Jesus with Jerusalem and Zion showing of his power and preaching to sprits in there humanity telling them to have Faith and they must prepare their body for salvation to have eternal peace, and spirits that has no faith is for eternal damnation to face Death this made him hate Jesus more, God/Cain got some strong giant godly spirits and then they went where Elijah was staying and said they came to arrest him, Elijah asked is it for doing good? They bound Elijah in chains and brought him in prison.

The news flashed in the nations that Elijah is captured and is in prison there was much excitement among the godly spirits spreading the news from nation to nation victory to God of Israelites, god (Cain) began to torment Elijah saying you took my kingdom and am going to take it back, I am the first god of the earth and I deserve to be king in the kingdom and they began to flog Elijah with chains, the other godly spirits joined and began kicking Elijah saying its because of you we had to suffer in fire dying of thirst.

Elijah in the body never tasted death to be a Spirit

Israel was excited Elijah was apprehended in custody and went to the prison in haste and began to torture Elijah, with insults, you want Jerusalem to be your Queen, you gave her Isaac and don't accept me, I hate you.

Elijah said not a word and took all the punishment by the godly spirits, they spat at him slapped his face saying speak now show us your power, Elijah said not a word, you sent the devils to Hades and you can't open your mouth to say one word to save yourself.

The godly spirits said look at him who put fear in us and sent us to the devouring fire in Hades and ask us to repent in front of spirits in there humanity to humiliate us for our sins cannot say a word show us your power and we will let you go, Elijah kept his mouth shut, they began to kick an break his arms and through him in a dungeon, saying if we get Jesus to leave the earth we will rule all nations.

HADASSAH IN THE BODY OF MAGDALENE

Hadassah in the body of Magdalene queen of godly spirits she hated Elijah for destroying Babylon and sending her to suffer in Hades because she set the body of Zion and Jerusalem on fire she prepared a banquet for godly spirits, they came from everywhere and entered Jews and gentiles to celebrate the capture of Elijah.

The godly spirit Cain switch body and entered Herod and Israel switched body and entered Philip (PETER) other godly spirits switched bodies and entered the officials and Roman soldiers and made the spirits in there humanity none active.

The music started and Hadassah in the body of Magdalene seduced her spirit to do belly dancing for Israel her king and father and said to Israel now we shall be King and Queen of the earth. Israel and her preplan what she should do and say and started to belly dance for Cain in the body of Herod and got excited the music stopped and she fell at the feet of Herod and Cain spoke through the mouth of Herod and said ask me what ever thou wilt and I will give it thee.

Hadassah went to Israel in the body of Philip (Peter) and said what shall I ask? He said you know what we planned, and in haste returned and said the head of Elijah on a charger. Cain got scared in the body of Herod knowing Spirits don't die and Elijah will come after him, everyone looked at the godly spirit (Cain) in the body of Herod and he said to the soldier to bring the head of Elijah on a charger to me and she gave it Israel in the body of Philip (Peter)

Holy Spirits sleep after the body is dead, Elijah is now a Spirit without flesh and took this opportunity to take a rest till Jesus call his name to continue the work according to the Testament of CHRIST for Victory in the Kingdom.

JESUS AND ELIJAH AFTER HE WAS BEHEADED

Jesus went up the mountain after Elijah was beheaded to discuss his departure to hand over power to Elijah, Jesus said the mission is nearly finished have patience I won't be with this faithless generation much longer. They used the mountain to communicate.

When he came down the mountain, the crowd was waiting for him, they brought a man that was possessed with a godly spirit, they said Jesus have pity on him and help us, we asked your disciples to cast out the demon but they had no power to cast it out. Jesus said they have no faith.

Jesus asked the demon how long you been in this body the demon said through the mouth of the man since he was a boy. Jesus said come out from this man right now the demon threw the man on the ground at Jesus feet foam coming out from the man's mouth screaming have pity, Jesus said get out now and don't ever enter his body again, the demon gave a loud cry and came out leaving the man exhausted, Jesus said to the man stand to your feet and go your way. The disciples said why the demon did not leave him when we told him to go away. Jesus said its because you have no power over godly spirits.

A Jew in the crowd seeing the power of Jesus casting out the demon asked Jesus what do I have to do to have eternal life, I am not perfect, Jesus said none of you are perfect, follow me and you will know the truth why you can't go to heaven not even with all the money you have you can buy your way to heaven, it's difficult for spirits of gods in there humanity in the kingdom but they have a choice if they have faith in Elijah they will have eternal peace. The man asked how can I be perfect if I was are born not perfect, Jesus said it is impossible but If you have faith and prepare your Kingdom for salvation the Spirit created will enter heaven in perfection by WORD. Like Isaac.

Israel in the body of Peter said we followed you thinking there is hope for us from captivity? Jesus said you shall receive multitudes with no faith like you, only those who has faith in Elijah will have eternal peace on the days of salvation, Christ whose body you hanged will create perfect Spirits in kingdoms from the flesh of Zion and Jerusalem according to the Testament. Elijah promise to give you spirits from your seed if you fornicate with your mother before you took the law, you Know the scripture Elijah taught you before you went against Him.

You made a big error when you went against Elijah and CHRIST and put your hope in devils, spirit of gods don't enter heaven, you are not the Son of Elijah you are a god of god (Cain) Isaac is the Son of Elijah by the WORD

Jesus said Israel hear this while you are in the body of Peter, The Lord is Elijah and the only savior of spirits that has faith in him, If you had loved him he would give you eternal peace and He would create in your kingdom a Spirit through Christ to be his Son, he taught you scripture but you envied his greatness, there is none greater than

Elijah the Lord of the earth. Israel said you are right there is no other but Him that could save me and never asked Jesus any more questions

THE HEBREWS SONS OF ELIJAH AND JERUSALEM

A Jew said to Jesus a Hebrew is casting out demons in your name, we told him to stop because he is not a Jew. Jesus said don't stop him if he do miracles like me the truth is he is a Christ he is not a Jew if any one attack my people it is better to put a stone around his neck and cast himself in the sea.

The Hebrews brought their children for Jesus to bless them, the demons in the disciples got jealous and seduce them to tell the children to go away, Jesus said don't stop them, I want the children to come to me for they are Righteous in the kingdom, and will enter heaven. Jesus said any one who is not like them will need salvation to have eternal peace if they have faith.

Jesus said to Jerusalem in the body of Mary your children through Isaac are blessed after I return to heaven many godly spirits in this generation will persecute them but they shall have eternal life as you well know they are Spirits of Christ of our Father.

The Jew asked Jesus why did you say these Hebrew's are Christ's, who gave you the authority to say that, we follow the law of our God and not CHRIST? Jesus replied I will ask you a question and answer me and I will tell thee why I am saying this. Elijah was he of creation or was he born from the seed of man? Tell me. He said I don't know.

Jesus said neither will I tell thee by what authority I say this when you see your God ask him why you are not a Christ. The godly spirit said which is the important of the two Testaments to follow the Testament of Christ or the testament with the law to Death.

Jesus said: Hear o Israel Elijah is the Lord and only Saviour, he saved you from birth and taught you scripture there is none greater than Elijah the Lord and he created Isaac by the WORD with Jerusalem. Isaac is not the son of the dead but Son of the living Spirit Elijah.

The godly spirit Israel in the body of Peter said, true. There is no other savior and he dear not ask Jesus any more questions to prevent the crowd from hearing the truth of Elijah and CHRIST to keep their names a secret.

THE TRANSFIGUARATION

Jesus went up the mountain. Israel in the body of Peter seduced Peter to stalk Jesus to see what Jesus was doing in the mountain and saw to his amazement Jesus transfigured himself in the Spirit and Elijah appeared in the mist and they both entered the mist and herd Jesus saying to Elijah the mission is finished the time has come to take over when I call your name.

Israel hid himself in a booth and kept what he had seen and heard his secrete from the other godly spirits. He Saw Elijah is alive who he rejected with other godly spirits that was wickedly like him and suffered and was thrown in prison, cut off Elijahs head, is a Spirit still on earth. He was in fear of returning to Hades.

THE BEGINNING OF THE BATTLE FOR THE EARTH

The godly spirits who followed Jesus was in the body of his followers was disappointed they realized what they did to Elijah there was no hope for them to remain on earth and planned to kill Jesus as the Passover and declare war against Elijah to rule the earth.

The godly spirit (Cain) in the body of Judas gathered a multitude of godly spirits in the nations to enter Jews and gentiles to capture Jesus. Israel/Godly spirit in the body of Peter and other godly spirits gathered in council to set up a plan to condemn Jesus so it will look like its Jews and mankind that Kill Jesus as spirits in there humanity can't see the godly spirits from captivity/

Cain/god in the body of Judas said to Israel/Godly spirit in the body of Peter I have a room arranged in the city for the Passover, invite Jesus to celebrate the feast with the other twelve humans he picked to follow him and I will wait with the multitude to pin him down with the net.

The evening came and the twelve Jesus had picked to follow him sat at the table waiting for him. When Jesus arrived he looked at them and said one of you seating on the table is going to betray me, each said it is not I, who is it? Each said is not I. Jesus said my mission is finished according to the Testament of CHRIST of what you will do and what Elijah will do, It is better my betrayer had not been born.

Jesus took a loaf of bread and said you are all of the same seed, He broke it in a small pieces and said you are like these small pieces from the same seed in the flesh, He took a cup with blood and said you were born in flesh with blood and handed the cup to them to drink. Then said I will sacrifice body and my blood you will spill to establish the testament of CHRIST for all spirits from the seed of god in there humanity that has faith to have eternal peace.

Israe/Godly spiritl in the body of peter said though the other godly spirits will reject you I will not renounce my faith. Jesus said I can assure you this very night you will, befor the cock crows you will say I did not cast you out from the same body with Jerusalem,and thaught I was the CHRIST

Jesus said to God I shall not be in your company again, and all of you will renounce your faith and crucify me but on the third day I will rise and return to my Father who sent me to tell Mankind the Truth that is hidden from them. Israe/Godly spiritl in the body of Peter was scared knowing Elijah is going to come after him said even if all godly spirits renounce their faith I shall not do so.

After Jesus was through speaking he said to the godsly spirits what they will do, Jesus said my mission is finished and was his way out. His betrayer god/Cain in body of judas with multitude of godly spirits from captivity signal Jesus is leaving the apartment, as Jesus came outside they cast a net over him and took him away in captivity, the godly spirits seducing the disciples fled from the diciples to put Jesus on Trial to leave the Earth to rule the earth.

THE TRIAL BY GODLY SPIRITS

The council of godly spirits gathered Jews and gentiles to seduce them to be false witnesses to give evidence against Jesus to condemn him to leave the earth.

After the godly spirits tseduce the Jews and gentiles to say this or that through there mouth as false witnesses they brought Jesus out from the dungeon in the temple to face Israel/God in the body of Peter.

The first witness seduced by a godly spirit came forward and said Jesus said he will pull down this temple made by human hands and build another not made with hands. Israel/God said through the mouth of peter what have you to say about this evidence against you. Jesus said not a word? Israel/God said through the mouth of Peter so you have no answer? Jesus kept silent, made no reply whatever.

"Jesus can see God/Israel is a godly spirit just like he can see Jesus but the witnesses have no clue what is going on in this Spiriual showdown Jews and gentiles are pawns in this trial as they can not see spirits while they are in there humanity. The difference Jesus is manifest to be seen by spirits in there humanity while the godly spirits have to possess bodies to seduce spirits in there humanity to lead them astray."

The God/Israel said : Jesus what have you to say to these charges made against you by these witnesses? Jesus made no reply.God/Israel got angry and tore the garment of peter and asked the godly spirits what should we do? The godly spirits shouted through the mouth of Jew and gentiles Jesus should die so we can live on earth to rule in kingdoms.

They began to spit on Jesus and curse and covered his face and began to strike Jesus with fist of those they seduced saying prophesy what will happen to godly spirits, Hadassah in the body of Magdalyn said to God in the body of Peter I saw you following Jesus, God/Isrel said to Hadassah in the body of Magdalyn I don't know this man, the cock crowed, Hadassah said but you were with others godly spirits following Jesus, God said I don't know him. Jesus made Peter see and hear preventing Israel from using his eyes and unblocked the ears of Peter the cock crowed again. Israel/God began to curse through the mouth of Peter and god/Cain in the body of Judas and other godly spirits had a council meeting to let Pilate judge Jesus to make Jews and mankind take the blame for crucifying Jesus, the council decided for all the godly spirits in the nation to enter the body of Jews and gentiles to cry loudly to Pilate to crucify Jesus.

god/Cain in the body of Judas wanted to be King of the earth and went in the body of Pilate blocked his eye and ears, to judge Jesus. The godly spirits of God/Israel don't want god/Cain to be the King of the earth and want to be the King of the earth God/Israel want god/ Cain to take the blame for passing his godly seed to him for not being perfect and making Jews not perfect like Hebrews and want Elijah to send him back to Hades so he can be King of the Spirits on earth.

THE godly spirits set up Jesus to look like a lunatic they took his clothes off and put a purple robe on him took thorns twisted it around and made a crown and stuck it on his head, put a staff in his hand and began to mock and laugh through the mouth of Jews hail king of the Jews when they had enough of their mockery they led him away jesus to god/Cain in the body of Pilate for judgment.

THE TRIAL BY PILATE

They brought Jesus to be tried by Pilate: Pilate said what wrong has he done? the godly spirits said through mouth of jews we want you to judge this man for us for calling himself the king of the Jews and causing a lot of disturbance in the nation with a new religion to have faith and the kingdoms of gods is for salvation, we follow the law of our God and don't know where he came from.

Pilate said what am I suppose to do with this man you say is a king of the Jews? The godly spirits shouted through the mouth of Jews crucify him louder and louder crucify him. Pilate asked Jesus, are you the king of the Jews? Jesus said, God told you to say this. Pilate said am I a Jew? What have you done to offend the Jews in the nation? are you a Jew? He got no reply from Jesus.

Pilate said this man you say is the king of the Jews judge him by the laws of your God. The godly spirits seducing the Jews to shouted louder and louder crucify him, god/cain in Pilate told the guards to take the man away and have him flogged.

They took the robe off Jesus and began to flog him with the cane, spat on him and began mocking Him he made godly spirits cry now he can't say a word to save himself, they brought Jesus back for to Pilate he said I find no fault in this man they shouted louder and louder crucify him. Pilate wrote Jesus king of the Jews you shall be crucified. After the godly spirits left the body of the Jews they possessed. and said Jesus is not king of the Jews. Israel is our King.

JESUS ON THE CROSS SANCTIFIED IN THE BODY (MT.28.12-14)

After they nailed Jesus to the cross they shouted let us see if CHRIST will come after the King of Israelites so we may believe CHRIST exist, they flung taunts at Jesus, make CHRIST come from heaven to save you. Jesus was bleeding drop after drop of blood on earth to Passover the WORD to Elijah to continue the work for salvation of kingdoms from the flesh of Jerusalem at the appointed time for CHRIST to create Spirits in Kingdoms for salvation according to the Testament in the Tabernacle

It began to get dark over the nation as the last drop of blood was about leave the body of Jesus he called Elijah, Elijah and and His Spirit separated from His body, Jesus was now a Spirit without flesh and He went to Join Zion, Jerusalem and Elijah. Jesus said to them my mission is over those who followers me did not Know of CHRIST to accept Him as a Creator, Israel and the godly spirits wanted to know if I was the CHRIST the Spirit of Adam he hanged on the tree when he was human he wanted to keep the name of CHRIST and Elijah a secret to mislead mankind astray to worship him as the mighty God who created them to have control in the kingdoms with spirits of gods in there humanity.

Jesus said to Elijah when I called your name on the cross Israel said let us see if CHRIST will come and take him down from the cross. Jesus said to Elijah Israel/God did not realize I passed the WORD to you to continue the work for final Judgment to establish the Kingdoms for Salvation at the appointed time.

The Jews that took the body from the cross and put the body of Jesus in cave and rolled a stone at the entrance of the cave did not know scripture to know my Spirit was now separated from the body they crucified on the cross, Jesus said to Zion, Jerusalem and Elijah I am happy to be a Spirit to spend a few days with you before I return to Father and leave you on earth. Elijah: you are the Judge everything is now in your hands.

Jesus said to Zion and Jerusalem I told the spirits in there humanity the truth before judgment begin in Kingdoms from your flesh to prepare themselves for Salvation to have eternal peace and must have faith in you before CHRIST return to create Spirits in kingdoms according to the Testament in the tabernacle. what He will do on the days of Salvation

Elijah went to the cave in the night and took the body of Jesus from the cave and brought it for Zion and Jerusalem to prepare and put it next to the body of Elijah to take to heaven to be in the tabernacle as a remembrance according to the prophecy of the ETERNAL what Christ will do and what Elijah will do if the devils made a god in this world.

The godly spirits was in suspense and in fear Elijah will return them to Hades, the godly spirits came out of the body of the Jews and ran away and possessed bodies of mankind in other nations. They said let the Hebrews (the people of Jerusalem and Elijah) populate will capture them after and make slaves off them.

Peter remembered Jesus saying he will rise the third day got curious went to the tomb and rolled the stone at the entrance of the cave to see if Jesus was in the tomb and saw the strip of cloth that was around Jesus on the cross laying on the ground ran out of the tomb in fear, and told the Jews they came in the night and took the body Jesus .

WITH MY BODY THEY SHALL ARISE (IS20.11)

After the body of Jesus was taken down from the cross, there was flashes of lightning, rumblings with thunder in the nations on earth and earthquakes breaking down buildings, hail stones falling from the sky falling on the temples followed by wind and rain for three days, the godly spirits was in fear in the nations, inhabitants in the nations crying thinking it's the end of the world crying to God to save them.

Jesus said to Elijah I will see what the WORD will do when I am not on earth, the time has come to return to Father: Jesus said to Zion and Jerusalem; my Sister while you are still on Earth Elijah will protect you, I have come to the end of the mission CHRIST sent me to do with Elijah for Him to create Spirits in kingdoms from your flesh to make everyone on earth holy equal and accepted in heaven.

Jesus said I leave you in peace, while you are still on earth, do not let your heart be troubled and have grief because I am leaving you to return to CHRIST, but when Elijah resurrect you will rejoice I love you my Mother and Sister and Brother they hugged each other there was pillar of clouds over the nations. Jesus picked up his body, held it in His hands and started to walk on air to the pillar of cloud over the nation.

BLESSED ARE THE SPIRITS THAT SLEEP THEY SHALL ARISE (DEUT.28.4:PS132.11)

Elijah commanded the Spirits of Jerusalem through Isaac (Hebrews) that sleep in the nations on earth to wake up and rise to the cloud to go to heaven and follow Jesus. The Spirit of Isaac came took the body of Elijah and multitudes of Spirits from his seed (Hebrews) that slept in the earth in the nations started walking on air to the clouds over the nations, the godly spirits saw this spectacular of multitudes of Spirits coming out from the earth and walking up to the clouds over the nations while they are on earth waiting for judgment made them angry and Jealous.

Jesus got in the cloud and the multitude of the Spirits of Hebrews got in the pillar of cloud over there nations Elijah commanded the Spirit of the winds to come unto the cloud with Jesus and Spirits in the pillar of cloud in the nations to follow Jesus on the cloud to the tabernacle in heaven and they vanish from sight.

THE ARRIVAL OF JESUS IN HEAVEN (DEUT.32.2:MT27.52REV15.3)

Jesus arrived in heaven with clouds after clouds with Hebrew Spirits in the tabernacle to meet CHRIST on the throne and said all these are from Jerusalem and Elijah great and marvelous are his deeds Father before you in the tabernacle Just and true are his ways and resurrected multitudes of Spirits in your Name as a testimony in the tabernacle

Jesus and his Brothers and Sisters and Angels assisted these new Spirits from the earth with apartments Jesus had built before His mission on the earth to enjoy the everlasting life prepared for them their needs when they came to up to heaven of heavens receive blessing from the ETERNAL SPIRIT IN THE LIGHT.

THE godly spirits from captivity spread out in the nations and went in the bodies of mankind and began to possess there body they could see through their eyes of the spirits in there humanity and hear with there ears and seduced the spirits in there humanity to make images to worship them, possessing there body the spirits in there humanity began to carve gods in wood, stone, silver and gold the spirits in there humanity began to do witchcraft in the nations there godly spirits startted to seduce there spirits in humanity indoctrination in religion to do magic to have control the people until they are dead to be like them.

ZION, JERUSALEM AND ELIJAH TOOK REST

Elijah said to Zion and Jerusalem after Jesus and the Spirits of Hebrews went up to heaven, Jesus and I was sent to cast out Cain and Israel from the same body as you and manifest in the flesh I got Satan and the godly spirits released to repent for rape and murder my head was cut off by Cain.so he and Israel could reign as kings of the earth.

Jesus told the spirits in there humanity to have faith in me and to prepare their kingdom for salvation to have everlasting peace and to be aware of godly sprits in their body and they crucified Him, Cain and Israel and multitudes of godly spirits was released from captivity to warn Jews and Gentiles of the chaos in Hades and to have faith to rest in peace so they don't end in Hades like them instead of doing what they were released to do, to go all over the earth to seduce the spirits from there seed to have faith to have to rest in peace, instead they seduce the spirits in the body they possess to do like the devils of ancient times to pass on their seed to make gods to worship them with all kinds of religion to mislead to have control in the Kingdom.

Jerusalem said Elijah our children are in danger if the godly spirits remain on earth they will want to kill every Hebrew on earth as they killed my brothers in the beginning and will rape our daughterss to make gods Elijah Jerusalem said; send them back to Hades.

Elijah said everything has to be justified for peace so far they have kept away from our Hebrews, they are responsible for saving their children from ending with Death Jesus was crucified for telling their children what they have to do for their peace, further more I save their forefathers in the vessel in the flood and told them to tell their children to have faith for peace. Jesus came to confirm this message to their children they must have faith, and about salvation and crucified Him thinking he was the CHRIST.

Elijah said to Zion and Jerusalem let us take a rest while the earth is populating with Hebrews, the spirits of gods are multiplying Kingdoms until salvation end. Elijah said to Zion and Jerusalem when you awake from sleep you shall resurrect to heaven to be with CHRIST to see the battle for the earth and final judgment on devils and godly spirits.

There was peace on earth for a while, the earth was populating with all kinds and sizes short, tall, fat, slim the godly spirits doing the same as Judah when he was human in Babylon interbreeding people to lookalike as there creation and branding them with marks on their body.

Zion and Jerusalem awake from sleep and lived among the Hebrews in a town Zion lived on her own in a house, Jerusalem lived in a small town in a house in a field away from Jerusalem The godly spirit (Cain) found out where Zion was living and approached her with hate and said I've come to set a trap for you to go to Hades to sin with devils, Zion said CHRIST rebuke you, he said Christ is in heaven I am the king of the earth now and everyone one earth live by the law of devils. He said since Jesus left the earth everything is the same and we have not seen Elijah since we beheaded him.

Zion felt threatened by Cain/god, she called Elijah loudly, wake up from sleep Cain/god is threatening my life he said he is setting a trap for me to sin with devils in Hades. Elijah appeared and said you are threatening Zion's life to be with devils. Cain said I am the king of the earth now and everyone must live by the law.

Elijah said the earth must have one King. Elijah commanded the Spirit of the Sun to pull up god (Cain) from the earth to the gate of the Sun and let him fall to meet the King of devils and Death in consuming fire for rape and murder.

Zion said thanks Elijah let me be in your presence to have peace since he returned from Hades he had been provoking me, his threats was more than I could bear it was righteous to remove him from the earth, now when I go out godly spirits are threatening my life.

Zion said: Elijah my flesh is my inheritance on earth and the godly spirits is destroying it with disease and there will be no kingdoms that is good for salvation unless you remove the godly spirits from the earth, daily Zion cried to Elijah to make supplications to CHRIST for her to go to heaven for CHRIST to give her children in Kingdoms for salvation before all her flesh go to waste by godly spirits.

Zion said Elijah: if the devil did not leave heaven and come to earth there would be no gods on earth to threaten my life. I was raped by Satan and made a god to be born in sin of a devil. I cannot take the blame for this sin I want to go to heaven so I can ask Angels to have mercy on me for making a god on earth.

Zion said to Elijah the Angels had knowledge if a god was born with the Eternal's creation it is forbidden and it would bring a god in the world to face Death, Zion said, Elijah I am humiliated I feel abused with this rape. Jerusalem and I have suffered in smoke and fire, our body was burnt to ashes you saved our Spirit and we are still on earth.

Zion said, Elijah Jerusalem and I should be in heaven living among Angels, Elijah you are my witness from ancient times and seen my suffering, you saved me and my daughters, our homes were burnt and taken in captivity by devils, in all my trials I have faith in you to resurrect me to heaven to CHRIST on the Throne in heaven.

THE FEAST IN THE TABERNACLE IN HEAVEN

Angels from all worlds made their way to the Tabernacle for annual feast. CHRIST sat on the Throne and all his Sons and Daughters from the earth and the new arrivals of Hebrews and their the children of Jerusalem and Elijah (Hebrews) seating among the angels from other worlds.

Jesus explained to the angels why there was a delay in creating Spirits In kingdoms for salvation and why CHRIST has not returned to earth to create Spirits in Kingdoms for salvation from the flesh of Zion and Jerusalem. The ETERNAL gave his blessings to CHRIST and all the Angels in the Tabernacle and Spirits in the Light on earth.

Christ told Jesus to read the Testament on salvation to the angels in the tabernacle, Jesus explained salvation cannot begin until the earth is fully populated with spirits of gods to save those who have faith and return the spirits that has no faith to Death for all in the kingdoms on earth to be same as angels in heaven created by the WORD.

Jesus said Zion and Jerusalem is still on earth with Elijah and can't leave the earth as all flesh on earth is their inheritance, they can't leave until judgment is passed on the devils and godly spirits threatening to destroy their flesh to rule the earth.

Jesus said My Mother made a god, she has suffered much for this sin and according to the testament, she must seat on the mercy seat to be judged by all Angels before CHRIST on the Throne before He can begin his work in creation though Elijah with the WORD for righteous Judgment.

Jesus said this is the reason my Father sent me to earth with Elijah to give the gods in there humanity a choice to have faith for eternal peace and to prepare their Kingdom for salvation for CHRIST to create Spirits in righteousness and for Satan and godly spirits to repent for rape and murder before Judgment begin on devils by Elijah according to the Testimony by the Eternal What CHRIST will do and what Elijah will do if the devils made a god with His Creation.

After Jesus was through speaking there was silence. The voice of Elijah was herd in the Tabernacle and the satellite system was switched to earth. Elijah looked up from Earth and all angels looked on the screen in the tabernacle, Elijah said CHRIST my holy Father, you created me to be a judge for the whole Earth and to save Spirits and resurrect them to you in heaven and to minister kingdoms for salvation from the flesh of Zion to create Spirits to live among Angels in heaven.

CHRIST said to Elijah what is your request my Son, Elijah said the people I saved in the vessel has populated the earth with multitude of kingdoms with spirits of gods. The godly spirits of the fall of Babylon and the flood that is released from Hades are threatening Zion and Jerusalem and want to destroy their flesh to rule the Earth with their spirits.

There is abundance of kingdoms all over the earth in this generation from the people I saved in the vessel and the godly spirits are spreading all kinds of disease from Death in their flesh so unless Zion see salvation there will not be any flesh that is good for salvation The godly sprits boast they will spread disease until there is no flesh left that is healthy for you to create Spirits in Kingdoms to live in heaven, they are angry spirits saying they did all the hard work screwing to make kingdoms and all that is on offer is everlasting peace for their sweat.

Holy Father Zion cries daily and would like the godly spirits removed from the Earth and for salvation to begin and ask for judgment on godly spirits for threatening her on Earth, can I have your permission to resurrect Zion and Jerusalem to seat on the mercy seat to give full account of the sin of the devil in this world to make a god so she can be judged by the Angels in the Tabernacle. Zion cries daily and say life without you is like carrying the whole earth burdened with sin on her shoulder and to be with you is pure happiness.

Elijah said Zion is suffering for your love as you for her, both of you are no more human but created Spirits to be together for Eternity to rule all worlds in the universe this suffering is worse than Death in hell, my Holy Father accept my plea for mercy so there be peace and harmony between you forever through Faith peace and love.

After Elijah asked for mercy and asked for Zion to be tried by Angels in the Tabernacle there was silence and all Angels looked at CHRIST and he said, Elijah my Son your way is righteous for peace and harmony in the worlds, I will send Jesus to bring her up, you know what to do, command a pillar of cloud to come where you are with Zion and Jerusalem and Jesus will be waiting to take her up to the tabernacle.

Elijah said to Zion Jesus is coming to take you up to heaven prepare yourself for the journey, Zion said thanks my savior and warrior, when I enter heaven I will rejoice and speak of your marvelous achievement and righteous judgment and mercy and patience to give Christ the Victory in the battle in the Kingdom.

Zion said: Elijah I am happy for you and Jerusalem and all your children populating on earth though Isaac your blessed Son by the WORD now in heaven, Elijah at last my hour is coming to leave the earth I give you praise for all you have done for me since CHRIST created you to finish the work in salvation to give all who have faith in you eternal peace, and to put an end to spirits born in sin to suffer Death

Zion said: Elijah I know CHRIST love you and listen to you, you are faithful and perform all that is required of you in the Trinity by the WORD for righteous Judgment.

ZION LEAVES THE EARTH FOR HEAVEN (REV10.1:REV11.12:MT24.30)

Jesus arrived and waited it the pillar of cloud, she gave Jerusalem a hug and said I love you my daughter, gave Elijah a hug and said I love you they said give the Eternal and CHRIST and our brothers and sisters our love and wish them love and Happiness, Zion came out of the body She was in and was now in the Spirit and began walking on air toward the pillar of cloud to meet Jesus, when she arrived they hugged each other waved good bye and went into the cloud.

Elijah commanded the Spirits of the wind to come unto the cloud with Zion and Jesus and take them to the Tabernacle in heaven to CHRIST. Her Sons and Daughters with CHRIST, Isaac and his Sons and daughters and multitude of angels waiting to see Zion the most beautiful Spirit created by the ETERNAL.

Jesus brought Zion to the tabernacle to seat before Christ and multitude of angels inside the Tabernacle from other worlds and every one looking well dressed with designer outfit well groomed and looking at the most beautiful Spirit from the earth seating naked on the mercy seat. Zion began to cry, there was silence her daughter brought her a kerchief to wipe the tears, she composed herself looked at the Angels and said the devil left heaven and came to earth and he raped me and I conceived his accursed seed and gave birth to a god born in sin.

Zion said: His god brought much sorrow to me, he slay the body of Jesus, who is my witness in the tabernacle and raped my daughter Jerusalem in her humanity and she conceived and gave birth to a god as wicked as the god of Satan and became a tyrant on Earth.

The son of god imitated the devils cast out of heaven that came to Earth, became a prophet under oath to teach gods to live to Death. The son of god hanged the body of CHRIST so he could be a king with the devils. CHRIST is my witness in the Tabernacle and also my Sons and Daughters in the Tabernacle.

The devils raped my Daughters and burnt our houses my sons and daughters are my witnesses to all what the devils did on earth and are my witnesses in the Tabernacle.

THE DEVILS LEFT HEAVEN TO BE SINNERS ON EARTH

Zion said to the Angels,Satan came to earth I asked him what he is doing on earth he said he is Angel and was sent by the ETERNAL to teach Adam to do gardening and to protect me and Adam from Death, he held me I pushed him away from me, he slapped me, I fell on the ground and he forcefully raped me and took my virginity and I conceived his accursed seed and gave birth to his god born in Sin through no fault of mine.

Zion said to the Angels I never saw a devil to know he was not an Angel of the Eternal's Creation or to know what a devil looked like, I knew when he touched me it was not righteous to lay his hand on me and pushed him away. I did not know what sin is, or knew he was an enemy of Angels, I did not know what a devil is or know where he came from, I felt unclean when he put his hand on me I pushed him away from me and as I was about to call Adam he slapped me and I passed out.

Zion said I was created with CHRIST, by the WORD and not through Sin. I had no pleasure in this sin. I gave birth to a god from the seed of a devil on earth with much pain and sorrow. Christ is my witness in the tabernacle.

The devil is the first rapist on Earth he strangled his god and kidnapped my daughter while she was pregnant for his god. Satan held my daughter in captivity to make gods for him. The son of god eliminated all my Sons on Earth and held Jerusalem in her humanity in captivity to make Israelites for him after the devils was removed from the face of the earth to Hades to await punishment By Elijah for rape, murder, and kidnap.

The Angels were in shock to hear of the sins of the Devils with holy daughters of Zion and CHRIST in there humanity. Tears began falling from their eye.

Zion cried I felt unclean after my body was burnt to ashes to be live in the body of an old woman for peace. My flesh is multiplying spirits of gods passing on the seed of devils of Death and also multiplying kingdoms for salvation.

There godly spirits nailed Jesus on a cross for telling their spirits the truth and to be weary of false teaching and worship to lead many astray, Jesus told them they must have faith to have Eternal peace and to prepare their body for salvation to have a Spirit of creation.

Elijah released the godly spirits in Hades to warn their spirits in there humanity of the chaos in Hades and to have faith in Elijah to save them from everlasting fire. Instead they enter bodies and seduce their spirits to commit more sin and want to destroy my flesh and Jerusalem so they can rule the earth with godly spirits.

Zion said I have suffered more than I can bare, I've seen corruption and violence by devils and godly spirits and I am the one who is blamed for sin, and not the devil that left heaven to rape me and my daughters to make gods to rule the earth and are planning to declare war against Elijah and CHRIST for the Earth.

Zion gave the Angels a full account of the wickedness of devils before they were removed to Hades and the desire of godly spirits on earth wanting to destroy flesh by war and disease to prevent CHRIST from creating Spirits in kingdoms for salvation. Zion said all flesh on earth with spirits of gods is my inheritance and it is burdened with sin and is becoming cancerous with the disease of Death. Therefore CHRIST my LORD while I seat on the mercy seat I ask you to begin salvation to remove every sprit from the seed of gods of the devils in Kingdoms from my flesh to the last seed to of Death.

Zion looked at the Angels, they were stunned overwhelmed with shock, some had there hands over there mouth, others were sobbing in horror hearing what the devils did, Zion said the devils raped my daughters they are holy women, they are in the tabernacle as my witness, Satan kidnap my first daughter and kept her in captivity to make gods, the devils set our homes on fire, cutting off the heads of my Sons, there gods set fire to my body, the godly spirits was threatening my life blaming me because they are not born perfect. Elijah saved Jerusalem and me from these godly spirits.

The Kingdoms have become corrupt with the spirits of gods possessed by godly spirits leading many astray in all kinds of religion to confuse and lead many astray in false worship of gods made of stone and wood as there god to live to Death. All this flesh is going to waste because of false worship and living according to the laws of their god in their nation.

Some of the Angels had their heads in hand sobbing, some were fainting never imagined there was so much evil in the world Zion prevailed over all this horror to be in heaven tell it as is to date. Zion went on telling the Angels of the full story of her life to judge her as an innocent nothing less.

Zion gave the Angels a lecture and said, I want everyone in the Tabernacle to listen to me clearly I was created under no law or to live under no covenant or was not told about devils and Death, I was created pure by the WORD and I am a Spirit same as everyone in Heaven I was created different from you to live in my image in the flesh I am no more in my Image but a Spirit like you, I am a virgin my Spirit did not commit sin, I have not had spiritual sex like you in heaven. I was not raped in the Spirit but in the flesh which was burnt to ashes.

Zion said I am not seating on the mercy seat in the flesh but the way I was created in the Spirit to tell you the truth about what is good and what is evil on Earth which you have not experienced by devils, you have escaped from making gods in heaven. I Bless the ETERNAL for casting the devils from heaven to prevent Angels from giving birth to gods in heaven.

You would have to go through the torment and trials of Faith and Love, I have never stopped loving my CHRIST, He is a good husband even though this god was born in sin CHRIST brought him up the good way but he turned out to be a vagabond like a devil on earth with evil in his heart to do wickedness to our family and his god turned out to be more wicked than him and behaved like a tyrant putting fear on all on earth to worship him as a Mighty God.

Zion Said I did not come to heaven to commit sin, this is my first time in heaven nor did I commit adultery to make a god to be a sinner I was very happy and in love with Christ even up to this minute my love has not diminished I am happy to be in heaven to be with CHRIST forever. I have explained to every Angel in the Tabernacle the circumstance in the way I became a victim and ask every Angel to have mercy on me, and I shall forgive everyone who called me a sinner, if I can't have your mercy banish me forever and all my flesh on earth let it be burnt to ashes.

Zion said my desire is to live the everlasting life with my CHRIST and to give me children in Kingdoms for salvation that is holy and pure on earth with everlasting life to populate in worlds without end in the universe.

THE FINAL JUDGMENT ON ZION

CHRIST sat on the Throne in the tabernacle looked at the Angels to judge Zion on the mercy seat for sin.

One Angel said Satan had lust for flesh he left the good life in heaven to go to earth to rape Eve to make a god to pass on the seed of Death in Zion's flesh, Satan is the sinner not Zion he and every devil who went to earth deserve to return to Death for rape.

Another Angel said Satan left heaven to earth to make a god in the flesh of Zion because he could not make a god in heaven and wanted to make a god his creation on earth, we know it was forbidden for any one in heaven to go to earth, he went to earth with full intention to rape Zion to make a god. Zion is not guilty of sin.

Another Angel said whoever the ETERNAL created is by the WORD and not in sin Satan knew it was unrighteous to make a god with the ETERNAL'S creation. To make a god to be born from the seed of devils is sin for Death. Zion is innocent of sin.

Jesus asked every Angel in the congregation in the tabernacle to put up their hands if Zion is guilty to give birth to a god in the sin of Satan? No Angel put their hands up to condemn Zion for sin.

Jesus asked every angel in the congregation in the Tabernacle to put up their hands if Jerusalem is a sinner to make gods for Satan in captivity? No angels put up their hands to condemn Jerusalem as a sinner.

Jesus said the Verdict by all Angels in the Tabernacle is unanimous Zion and Jerusalem is not guilty. Satan and the devils that went to earth are the sinners. According to the prophesy of the ETERNAL in the ark the devils were warned while they were in heaven if any devil made a god with the ETERNAL'S creation that His CHRIST would create His Elijah that would be stronger than any god they made and would pass judgment on every devil to return to Death for making a god in sin.

Jesus said Elijah is the Judge on earth and will pass sentence on the devils for rape, kidnapping Jerusalem in her humanity to make gods, Arson, Tyrannous hate on holy people of Zion and CHRIST while they were on earth in there humanity, and on godly spirits for threatening Zion and Jerusalem and setting fire on their body, attempting to kill Isaac Son of Elijah by the WORD and for murder for crucifying Jesus and killing Elijah in his humanity telling the spirits the Truth.

The Angels shouted an eye for an eye and tooth for a tooth Elijah let them all fall in the everlasting fire in Armageddon to return to Death

There was much joy in heaven the angels shouted CHRIST return to Earth and root out the spirits in the Kingdoms for Salvation and let Elijah send all that are anti Christ and have no faith in him to Death. Some Angels began to cry we want Justice for Zion and Jerusalem

Other Angels went up to Zion and said O Zion you have experience of what is good and evil we never knew existed and have suffered pain we have not suffered and worthy to be our Queen with CHRIST and be happy for ever to rule with Him on the throne of the Universe and have dominion in all worlds everyone in the Tabernacle was happy and said CHRIST reign forever.

Zion said Holy ETERNAL forgive me, Satan raped me and I gave birth to a god and he was born in sin, in holy flesh forbidden to devils.

The ETERNAL thundered from the heaven of heavens, my daughter mercy is granted thee. Your faith and love for CHRIST has brought you to heaven. I created thee with CHRIST to sit on the throne in heaven to be a Creator of Spirits when you are in heaven with my blessings. This sin of the devil will erase when CHRIST remove spirits of gods from kingdoms from your flesh to create Spirits until Salvation ends to the last seed of devils of Death.

Zion looked at CHRIST and said if I am worthy to seat next to you as your Queen let every Angel hear you say you love me forever. Christ said, Jesus bring your Mother to me, CHRIST held Zion in His arms he said I love you from the beginning, we were created together on earth as man and wife in the flesh now we are together in the Spirit, your King and Lord and Creator of Spirits to fulfill the prophesy of the ETERNAL what His CHRIST will do when Zion seat on the throne to Create Spirits in kingdoms for salvation from your flesh. The Angels shouted with joy Alleluia after they kiss.

CHRIST said to Jesus fetch me the Rings in the chalice made for me and your Mother before we were created and He put it on Zion's finger and said now we are Spirits created to be together for eternity. The angels came forward and bowed to CHRIST and Zion and gave them praise to Rule over them and celebrated for CHRIST to Create Spirits in Kingdoms for Salvation and feasted.

Their Sons and Daughters were happy and went to the palace to prepare Zion to go to the heaven of heavens with Christ to meet the ETERNAL and Arc Angels. Zion said to her daughters that slept in the earth and ascended and was her witnesses in the congregation said, let us give Praise to Elijah, He has been marvelous and kind and has turned my lamentation in sack cloth into wearing designer clothes for dancing, my Spirit is as clear as Light. I am innocent. Her daughters said Alleluia praise His holy name, Mother you are the most beautiful Angel the ETERNAL created and now you and Father is going to meet Him to receive His blessing to rule all worlds as King and Queen and Lord to create Spirits in kingdoms from the throne in Heaven.

The ETERNAL was happy to see CHRIST and Zion to communicate at his level as a creator of Elijah by the WORD to do holy work if a devil made a god. CHRIST and Zion spent some time with the ETERNAL Spirit in the Light and was served by Ark angels.

Ark Angels Michael gave CHRIST praise for Elijah His first Son in creation by the WORD with the WORD, Ark angel Gabriel said Elijah and is prudent and Judge with knowledge of the Trinity knowing what to do for peace and harmony, the communication between the Three of You is at the highest intelligence for every Kingdom on earth to have a Spirit in the light to be in heaven Zion said praise his holy name Elijah is my warrior and will save who has faith in him and not Anti CHRIST.

THE PROMISED SON BY THE WORD (HEBREWS MIC.4.10)

The people on earth of Jerusalem and Elijah through Isaac by the WORD with the seed of creation they are Spirits in the Light They don't need Salvation they can Pray Direct to CHRIST in heaven, the godly spirits call them Hebrews or saints, the Hebrews multiplied abundantly in the nations North East and North West of the earth they built cities with nice homes and successful in business and agriculture, Jerusalem lived in a small house in a field among them.

Elijah told Jerusalem when CHRIST come to pass Judgment on your enemy you will go to heaven with Him to see the final Judgment on the devils and godly spirits meanwhile I will have my rest while our blessed children are populating in peace.

THE ISRAELITES (JEWS JN.8.34-44)

There is a clear distinction: All Israelites are people between Judah, from the seed of god Cain) spirit name Israel and Jerusalem when she was human in the body of Babylon all spirits of gods in there humanity are the same spirit as Jews and need to prepare their body for Salvation to have eternal peace and for their body to be created with a Spirit in the Light by Christ to live in heaven through Elijah. Hebrews don't need salvation or religion to live by laws of ancients devils irrelevant to Spirits in the Light.

The Hebrews called the Israelites who worked for them in all manner of service as there servants Jews, meaning half breed, same Mother different father not Sons of Elijah and Jerusalem through Isaac with the Holy Seed to populate Immortal Spirits in the Light.

The godly spirits in the nations got together to discuss what to do the bodies they possessed to seduce the spirits in there humanity to lose faith and seducing them to make images of them in wood stone silver and gold to worship them as there god in the nation. Every nation had a god to worship and tattoo there body or slashed their body to be tribal.

The body the godly spirits possessed became diseased and the spirits in there humanity was in pain there heart failed them and their spirits separated after their body was dead, the spirits entered the body of the gods they possed doing the same as the seducing spirits in black magic and sorcery. They godly spirits never took heed of the preaching of Jesus and judgment if they don't warn spirits of the chaos in Hades.

THE kings of godly spirits gather together
to declare war to rule the Earth

One of the Kings of godly spirits in the body of the rulers in the council said, the Hebrews are building treasured cities, they have populated in abundance. Another King said the time has come to eliminate the Hebrew men from the earth so the Jews can rule the earth everything is the same since Zion left the earth. Another King said Jerusalem is on earth she calls the Hebrews with Elijah her blessed children they are the blesed humans of the earth.

Another king said, these upstarts don't want to mix and call us Jews and want to rule over us. Another King said let us declare war for the earth so we can rule with Jews in the nations like when Jerusalem was Queen of Babylon. Another king said our God created us to pass on his seed to make Israelites to rule nations on earth for all to live by his Law to Death. The Hebrews was not on Earth when he made us with Jerusalem in her humanity it is we Jews who should rule the earth we are on earth before the Hebrews of Isaac.

The kings of godly spirits agreed under oath to declared war on the Hebrews to eliminate there men from the earth and fight against Elijah for Jews to rule the earth. The godly spirits were jealous of the Hebrews of Jerusalem and Elijah and entered the body of the Jews and began to attack the Hebrews Jerusalem cried Elijah awake from sleep the godly spirits has declared war on our people the earth began to tremble to wake up Elijah. Elijah herd Jerusalem crying to save there blessed children.

THE WAGES OF SIN IS DEATH

CHRIST and ZION sat on the Throne in heaven, the Angels said to CHRIST we want Justice for Zion and Jerusalem the wages of sin is Death let us see Judgment by Elijah and the Spirit of the Sun on godly spirits for setting the body of Zion and Jerusalem on fire. The Tabernacle was full with Angels looking to see righteous Judgment on godly spirits for corruption and misleading spirits of gods in there humanity to worship them in the nations with false doctrine that lead to Death to prevent CHRIST from creating Spirits in Kingdoms for Salvation.

CHRIST said to Elijah proceed with Judgment you are the Judge, the son of god that hanged my body on the tree I want you to delivered his spirit in my hand.

The godly spirits in the nations declared war on Elijah, they went in the nations of the Hebrews and began to killed there men to prevent there men passing on the holy seed of Isaac to populate the earth with Hebrews and hold their women in bondage.

EPISODE 5

The Day Lord Elijah Judge Is Like A Thief In The Night (Num.16.30)

THE BATTLE FOR THE EARTH

Elijah sent pestilence in the nations and the people started to run inside their homes and locked themselves inside for days to avoid the pestilence. Elijah commanded hailstones with fire to fall on the homes in the Nations North to East of the earth the people began to run out of their houses on fire. Elijah commanded the wind to blow fire everywhere in the nations and the people was on fire the godly spirits came out of their body and tried to escape everyone was running here and there to escape from the nations.

Elijah commanded the Spirit of the Sun to pull up the godly spirits from the nations North to East from the earth and the spirits without flesh that has no faith and worship gods made of stone wood, silver and gold in the nations to join the godly spirits. The spirits was pulled up from the earth like a magnet pulling up dust by the Spirit of the Sun.

Elijah commanded the spirits of the Sun to pull up the godly spirits from the Earth that had no Faith and carry them to the mouth of the water and dropped the spirits in the mouth of the waters and they began to journeyed to the gate of Hades when the last spirit entered the gate was shut automatically never to await the final judgment. The people that escaped were few to populate to make kingdoms for Salvation.

Elijah gathered the godly spirits in battle for the Earth It was the first victory since the flood capturing the godly spirits and returning to them to Hades the Angels began to sing in the Tabernacle great and marvelous is the judgment on Elijah, true and Just are his ways, O Elijah your judgment is magnificent you deserve to be King of the Earth judging according to the Testament of CHRIST sending all who are wicked to the gate. The Daughters and Sons of CHRIST sang don't rest Elijah till Victory is accomplished.

OTHER Angels sang woe, woe, woe to the godly spirits among the inhabitants East to South of the earth. Elijah commanded pestilence of all sorts to go in the nations and every one ran into their homes for days then He commanded hailstones with fire to fall on homes in the nations North to South of the earth and commanded the wind to blow on the fire and there was bush fires everywhere in the nations.

The people began to run out of their homes the wind was blowing fire every where the people was on fire the godly spirits that possessed them separated themselves from the bodies they possessed. Elijah commanded the Spirit of the Sun to pull up the godly spirits separated from the body they posessed in the nations South of the earth. and drop them in the mouth of the waters, the godly spirits began to fall one on top each other in the mouth of the waters and began to journey to the gate of Hades to await the final judgment never to return to the face of the earth forever.

Elijah judges and makes war with the WORD that come out from His mouth it is mighty in battle to give CHRIST and Zion the Victory. The WORD break trees, create lightning, thunder, wind, hailstorms, clouds,clouds, rain,flood, create and bring destruction his wrath is quick the Spirit of the Sun wait for instruction by Elijah to fulfill what Elijah command in Judgment.

THE THIRD JUDGMENT DESTRUCTION IN THE NATIONS (JER.50.22:JOB.9.5)

The godly spirits in the nations South to West of the earth concentrated to seduce the spirits in there humanity to carve images of themselves in wood, silver, and gold to worship them as there god to mislead in religion and false worship to confuse the spirits in there humanity with false doctrine to worship them in temples and to give them false hope, built Pyramids for their spirits to enter the spiritual world.

Elijah commanded lightning, thunder and earthquakes to come and destroy all the temples and monuments of the godly spirits they worshiped gods in ntions, the tempest came and began to blow houses and trees and branches flying all over the nations followed by rain causing land slide, rivers running into their home taking away everything in its path.

There was a pause and mankind began to hate God for breaking up there homes in the nations, the body the godly spirits possessed began to have disease and break out in sores, and leprous and stink, there was dead bodies everywhere in the streets this created a problem for the godly spirits as there was few bodies and could be clearly seen by the Spirit of the sun with no flesh.

Elijah commanded the spirit of the Sun to pull up the godly spirits from the nations South to West from the earth and the spirits of the dead that worshiped the godly spirits as there gods.

Elijah commanded the tempest to come and take the godly spirits that was pulled up from the earth to the mouth of the waters and drop them, the sprits began to fall one on top each other in the mouth of the water and began to journey to the gate of Hades to await the final judgment, never to return to the face of the earth.

THE FORTH JUDGMENT BETWEEN ELIJAH AND ISRAEL AND HIS BATTALION (IS1.7 8: LK.21.20-21)

Israel and his battalion and multitudes of godly spirits in the kingdoms, he named them the dragons of the earth, fierce killers with authority to rule the nations and destroy kingdoms to prevent CHRIST from creating Spirits in Kingdoms from the flesh of Jerusalem if Elijah appear anywhere on earth.

Israel realized the godly spirits in three quarters of the earth was captured by Elijah and was in fear of returned to Hades, he declared war for the earth against Elijah knowing the time has come to face Elijah with the WORD with his battalion, Israel surrounded the nations with Hebrews with Jerusalem with his battalion of godly spirits he called them the dragons of the earth to eliminate every Hebrew on the earth and hold Jerualem hostage to be King on the Earth with Jerusalem as his queen to prevent her from going to heaven.

Israel found out Jerusalem lived in a cottage he entered the same body as her to hide from Elijah he began to cry: O Jerusalem my end has come let me stay in this body and we can live in peace together.

Jerusalem said, did the devils have peace on earth for f.>< . . . in my flesh, how can I have peace with you in this body. I have blessed children with Elijah and I am happy with him, get out from this body and go in the same body with your whore from Babylon who burnt my body to ashes, get out Jerusalem screamed at him you are malicious, stressful and violent and I don't want you in the same body as me.

Israel said, if you don't let me stay I will command my battalion to kill every Hebrew in the nations until you have no Hebrew to populate on earth, you can't get away from me I am your king as long as I am on earth if it's the last thing Ill do I will stay in the same body as you for making me not perfect or take you to the devils to punish you for making Israelites with me after they were removed from the earth. Jerusalem cried:Elijah, Elijah come and save me from Israel he entered the same body as me and threaten to kill every Hebrew in the nation with his battalion. Israel said Elijah you will not save me because I am still on earth living in this body instead of going to heaven and threaten to take me to Hades for the devils.

Jerusalem cried Elijah come to send this vagabond to god his father in the fire. Jerusalem herd in her ear now you shall see judgment on Israel for threatening you with devils in the fire in Hades.

JUDGMENT ON THE GOD OF ISRAELITES THE DAY HE ENTERS JERUSALEM (IS.1.7-8)

Elijah commanded the Spirit of the Sun to keep an eye on the house of Jerusalem in the field. Elijah looked up to the heavens and said CHRIST, my LORD, you wanted me to place your enemy in your hand the time has come to fulfill your wishes, CHRIST said vengeance is mine for hanging my body on a tree and eliminating My Sons from the earth and holding Zion and Jerusalem in captivity CHRIST said to ZION on the Throne watch and see,and CHRIST was on His way to earth, the Sons and Daughters joined Zion on the throne to look at this judgment

Elijah turned up at cottage of Jerusalem, when She saw Elijah she ran outside to meet Elijah she said Israel is in this body and is threaten me with Hades, Elijah said to Israel not by the might of your godly spirits in your battalion,you surrounded my people in the nations, but by my Spirit with the WORD I will send all of you back to Hades today from the face of the earth forever.

Elijah said: I have used restraint from punishing you and gave you a lot of time to warn the Jews of the chaos in hell and to teach them to have faith for eternal peace but you insist to bring shame on Jerusalem this Judgment is out of my hand CHRIST said vengeance belongs to Him.

Israel began to tremble in the body with Jerusalem in fear of coming out in danger of being caught by CHRIST. The angels in heaven began to say an eye for an eye and tooth for tooth take vengeance for us and keeping our Sister in captivity, Israel felt cornered if he tried to come out with no flesh he will be seen as a sinner he thought Elijah would have mercy and save him as a father to a adopted son to give more time on earth.

Israel took a chance came out of the same body with Jerusalem and tried to escape Judgment on him. The Spirit of the Sun pulled Israel from the Earth CHRIST caught hold of him he began to cry. CHRIST said I warned you not to hang my body on the tree I told you go and tell the devils to come and do the hanging you wanted to make a name for yourself on earth. Israel cried the devils told me to kill you and I will be a king with them to rule on earth, have mercy on me I have sinned he cried CHRIST said you disobeyed and condemned all from your seed if they don't have faith like you.

CHRIST took him to the lower region of Hades and cast him in with the devils in devouring flames in Hades the Judgment was justified on a sinful man (Lk.5.8) The prophet that perished when he ran out of Jerusalem (LK13.33) The Axe is ready to root out the sprits in kingdoms for salvation when Christ Return on the days of Salvation.

The godly spirits that had surrounded the nations of the Hebrews saw Israel carried away by CHRIST cried it can't be Israel is carried away from Jerusalem it was the first time they saw CHRIST and was in fear of returning to Hades. Elijah commanded hailstones with fire to fall on the houses in the nations West to North to flush out the godly spirits possessing the body of the spirits in there humanity.

Elijah commanded the Spirit of the Sun to pull up every godly spirit from the nations of the Hebrews, every one that was not a Hebrew was on fire in the nation running away screaming as soon as the godly spirits separated from their body they were pulled up from the earth by the Spirit of the Sun without flesh to remove them from the nations of the Hebrews to Hades.

Elijah commanded a tempest to come and carry the godly spirits to the mouth of the waters and drop them. The godly spirits began to fall one on top of each other in the mouth of the waters and journeyed to the gates of Hades. The queen of the devils counted the godly spirits took there names and put in the book of the dead for Death to await the final judgment. CHRIST sealed the gate of Hades and surfaced from the deep.

Elijah said Jerusalem now you will have peace from this stubborn rebellious son of god he did not want to obey he had a choice to have peace he did not keep to the scripture I taught him and chose to be a rebel to eliminate the Hebrews in the nations on Earth for his Israelites to rule with him. Jerusalem there is no point in staying on earth as the earth has to be repopulated with Jews and tribes from the remnants saved so prepare yourself to go to Heaven with CHRIST to be queen of all the people in the four corners of the earth with Spirits created by the WORD in kingdoms for salvation while you are in heaven.

The Hebrews and the remnants of the Jews and gentile tribes that survived will repopulate to make kingdoms for salvation and will have a choice to have eternal peace if they have faith while they live and prepare themselves for Salvation for the kingdoms on the Earth to be populated with righteous Spirits in the Light in Kingdoms for to be justified to be Queen of all righteous Spirits in Kingdoms on the Earth forever.

The devils and godly spirits are judged for leading mankind astray and are in captivity awaiting final Judgment to send them to Death In the everlasting Fire.

JERUSALEM RESURRECT TO HEAVEN (MT.27.52)

Elijah said Jerusalem the time has come for you to go to Heaven with CHRIST to be with Zion to receive a blessing from the ETERNAL and to be with your Brothers and Sisters and our Children to live among Angels in the worlds above.

Elijah said CHRIST our Father is waiting on the Cloud for you, they hug and kissed, she said thanks my King and she began to walk on air to the cloud to meet her Father it was the first time she was with CHRIST in the Spirit together.

Elijah commanded all the spirits of Hebrews in the Light that slept in the nations to ke up from sleep and Follow Jerusalem to the cloud to go to heaven,the Spirits woke up from sleep and out of the graves and began to walkk on air going to the clouds to meet Jerusalem this made CHRIST Happy seeing Jerusalem coming up to meet Him with multitude of Spirits in the Light.

Jerusalem got to the cloud and embraced CHRIST her FATHER then waved to Elijah and went in the Cloud. The Spirits of the Hebrews entered the cloud above the nations.

Elijah commanded the Spirits of the winds to come unto the cloud with CHRIST and Jerusalem and the clouds with Spirits in the Light above the nations and take them to the Throne in heaven with Zion.

This great spectacular was seen by angels CHRIST returning with Jerusalem with clouds after clouds landing Spirits in the Light from the Earth that has never been seen in the heavens the spirits from earth matching and waving their hands to Angels as they go to the tabernacle to register their names in the book of everlasting life.

THE PROPHECY OF THE ETERNAL OF WHAT CHRIST WILL DO AND ELIJAH WILL DO IF THE DEVILS MADE A GOD.

CHRIST created Elijah by the WORD to be with the WORD so spirits of gods who has faith in Elijah shall not be condemned and perish with Death but have everlasting peace and for spirits of gods in there humanity to prepare their kingdom for Salvation to be with a Spirit created with everlasting Life by the WORD

Elijah has Judged the devils and brought them to the lower region of Hades to await judgment for their wickedness so they can't have inheritance on the earth, the people from the seed of gods that remain in the nations on earth can now populate kingdoms in peace for Salvation, for their spirit to have eternal Peace. The godly spirits before the flood were captured and returned to captivity to await final Judgment for leading their spirits in the kingdoms astray in false worship.

Elijah had mercy on the remnants of Jews and tribes who were saved in the nations to repopulate on earth and will only save the spirits in the kingdoms that has faith in Him in the time of Salvation according to the testament of CHRIST to have ternal peace, And will not be condemned to Death.

REPENT

Elijah commanded Satan and the devils and godly spirits in Hades to go down on their Knee for coming to Earth to rape Eve to make a god in Zion's flesh, repent for murder, killing all the Sons of CHRIST in there Humanity, kidnapping Jerusalem in her humanity to make gods in her flesh, repent for hanging the body of CHRIST, repent for crucifying the body of Jesus.

Elijah commanded the fire in Hades to increase by the WORD to its maximum. The devils and godly spirits began to cry the earth began to tremble, and crack the devils and godly spirits began cry its enough we repent for all our wickedness, Israel cried Lord let me return to earth to warn the people to have faith if I returned from this heat they will believe me to save them from the devils, Satan held him by the throat and said mother fucker you sinned more than us while we are in this fucking heat you were having abomination with my Tamuze and want the Lord to save you from this fucking heat in Hades.

The godly spirits began to blame Israel,crying if you did not create us with Tamuze we would not be in the heat for your sin with our mother to be your creation, Satan said he did the same as us to create gods with Tamuze it is because of god his father we are cast out of heaven for sin.

The godly spirits began to cry to Israel if god your father did not rape our mother you would not be born to make us to be suffering in this heat with devils for your sin to pass on the seed of god of Satan to us, everyone in Hades was blaming each other for sin of the other and crying for Elijah to stop the increase of heat. The earth was trembling with all this crying in Hades and it brought on mountainous waves crashing on the shore of nations doing much damage.

A godly spirit cried Jesus said we should have faith or we will all perish, Jesus said he was sent to warned us not to teach false doctrine that lead to Death. Satan shouted in the heat we are all sinners from the seed of Death we had a choice like you fucking asses who prefer to be wicked like ancient devils fucking to make gods in holy flesh, now you want to have faith because your ass is in fire for doing the same as us fucking and passing the seed of Death, if we can't escape from this heat in Hades we have no chance to escape in this divouring fire in hell

A godly spirit cried if you devils did not provoke CHRIST and Elijah we would not be born in sin you left the good life in heaven to come to fuck in flesh like creatures on Earth. Satan cried I repent for raping Eve to make a god, for this one sin we were cast out of heaven now we are multitudes entombed in this fucking heat for rape, murder abomination and fucking holy women in captivity.

The devils shouted Satan this heat in Hades is wrath on sinners by the WORD with the Lord who removed us from the earth repent,

Satan cried who is the Lord, I do not know the Lord, the godly spirits cried he is Elijah he is the Holy One who sent us to be with devils he is the Judge, they cried repent Satan this heat is unbearable it is because you disobey and rebel against the ETERNAL we are suffering for your wickedness repent for your sin for making gods in this world, Satan cried I I I I re re re repent Lord ELIJAH I sinned with Tamuze and made a god with Eve.

Elijah commanded every devil and godly spirit in the fire to be on their knees and bless the ETERNAL HOLY SPIRIT, Bless CHRIST and Zion,Bless Jesus and Jrerusalem Bless THE SONS of ZION, all the Daughters of ZION and CHRIST, Bless Elijah Isaac and all his blessed SONS and Daughters on earth to live in the Worlds in the universe, without Death, Devils, godly spirits on earth and disease from Death for ever with your blessings.

The devils and godly spirits cried quickly we bless the ETERNAL SPIRIT, CHRIST and Zion, ELIJAH Jesus Jerusalem and every Spirit in the Light on earth to live forever without Death devils and godly spirits on earth forever with our blessings.

Elijah said to Israel don't hide nothing from the devils and tell them the truth: Who is Eve, Israel cried she is Zion ,Who is Adam He cried the CHRIST of the ETERNAL, who created his Elijah with the WORD, who is Abel? He is Jesus, who is Tamuze? He cried Lord She is Jerusalem, who is your mother, he cried lord have mercy she is Jerusalem who was in the body of Tamuze, tell the devils who is your father, he cried Cain the first god of Satan with Eve, tell the devils who brought you up from birth in the bush, he cried you Lord, tell devils the who taught you scripture, he cried you Lord Elijah.

The devils rushed on him, Satan called him deceiver with the Law another devil called him a dragon for flesh, another devil called him a falcon with the laws and commandments to live to Death. The devils were disappointed angry and crying you had all this knowledge you hanged Adam and made CHRIST escape from us they began to beat him with no mercy.

The godly spirits began to cry to the devils leave our father we are all corrupt you had knowledge of CHRIST when you were in heaven and knew if you made a god CHRIST would create His Elijah to cast you to the furnace to be with Death, stop beating our father because he told you the truth CHRIST was the Holy Spirit in the body of Adam. A devil said I am vex I am going mad because he did not tell us we could keep Adam alive to stay on earth and because of Truth we are in this fucking heat and allowed Christ to Escape from the earth to the Throne in Heaven, now he is looking at us as the scum of the earth and laughing at us devils and our gods making kingdoms for him to create Spirits in the Light.

Israel cried Elijah, Elijah save me the devils are attacking me he cried louder and louder Elijah, Elijah now I have Faith. Elijah thundered with the WORD for all to hear in Hades, you became stubborn, rebellious and did not keep to the scripture I taught you and provoked Me and CHRIST with war and abused Jerusalem when she was in Babylon to bring shame on her you were cruel to her and forgot who brought you up from the bush and fed you on milk and honey from the rock, you had a choice to have eternal peace for salvation of your body to be created with a Son to be like me in Salvation by the WORD

Elijah said to Israel you had no Faith when you had flesh on your spirit you are no more human and can't be born again, you hoped after you were dead to be a godly spirit to be a king of the spirits of the Earth with the devils so save yourself from them, you had knowledge of salvation to have eternal peace before you took the oath to live by the law of devils to Death and did the same to your mother as god your father and Satan and kept her in captivity under the Law in Babylon its to late to have Faith, mercy will be granted to spirits in there humanity who has faith and want eternal Peace, your choice was to be with devils and Death.

CHRIST AND ZION ON THE THRONE IN HEAVEN

Multitudes of angels came from many worlds to celebrate the Passover of power to CHRIST from the ETERNAL as a creator of Spirits in Kingdoms for Salvation when Zion seat on the Throne with CHRIST to make the covenant with the devils while they were in heaven Obsolete, for all Sprits in the Light to live by the new Testament of Christ without devils and godly spirits forever.

Angels from many worlds brought gifts to give CHRIST and Zion to celebrate and feast in the Tabernacle with them, there was much excitement CHRIST is going to make everything new in the worlds, the Angels were happy to see the beautiful angels of Christ and Zion from the earth among them in heaven and gave the ETERNAL praise for creating CHRIST and Zion to rule all worlds in the universe from the Throne in heaven, the Angels sang to CHRIST and Zion power is given thee O Lord of storm thunder and lightning to rule all Angels in the Light with excellence and Majesty on the throne in heaven

The ETERNAL gave CHRIST and Zion His blessing and said make everything New My Son now I shall have my rest from creation, then He blessed the Spirit of the Sun, Jesus and everyone in the ceremony and Elijah on earth waiting to Passover the kingdoms for CHRIST to create Spirits in kingdoms for salvation from the flesh of Zion and Jerusalem.

THE JUDGMENT ON DEVILS AND GODLY SPIRITS IN HADES (MT12.25MT13.30)

Multitudes of Angels came from many worlds to see the final judgment on devils and godly spirits for rape, murder, abomination, kidnap, arson, false worship to lead to Death. The Tabernacle was filled with Angels excited to see the final judgment between the Spirit of the sun and Elijah with the WORD.

Elijah thundered from the earth My Father I give you and Zion praise to seat on the Throne in Heaven with Majesty and Excellence. Eternal holy Father I bless you CHRIST and Zion to rule all worlds with Your mighty power. Your Majesty the time has come to execute final judgment on the devils and godly spirits to pass them over to Death so they have no inheritance on earth, so when you begin to create Spirits in the time of SALVATION it will asy to cast out spirits of gods in kingdoms for the final judgment on the spirits that has no faith for the Spirit of the sun to remove them from the earth to fall to the devils and Death. My Lord there are a few remnants of Israelites and gentile tribes left in the Nations and some are living among the Hebrews what should I do with them?

CHRIST thundered My Son don't root them out let them be for seasons to see the signs of salvation days and there hour of judgment in the kingdom. Elijah let them populate to make kingdoms on earth among the Hebrews when I return on the days of salvation it is to create multitudes of Spirits in Kingdoms for you and Jerusalem so all Spirits in the kingdoms will be in the Light to live in heaven. The spirits that are not in the Light when I cast them out on the days of salvation that has no faith in you and Anti CHRIST will not have rest, the other spirits of gods who have no respect for you as the Judge and King and a Lord of Lords you will return to the devils and the godly spirits in the fire till there are no more spirits of gods in the kingdoms to live to Death so it will be on earth as it was in the beginning without gods.

Christ said Elijah you can proceed to execute righteous Judgment on the devils and godly spirits from the earth to the gate of the sun, Elijah said Amen. The Angels sang woe, woe, woe, Alleluia, Jrusalem began to sing and clap her hands Elijah, Elijah, let me see judgment in heaven hallelujah. The Angels shouted alleluia, alleluia we give praise to Elijah for his wisdom to bring judgment on the Barbarians according to the plan of CHRIST. Jerusalem said Elijah make this dragon for my flesh fall and suffer in fire with his whore for making me and my Mother suffer in the fire in Babylon.

Elijah commanded the Spirit of the Sun to pull up every devil and godly spirit that surface the earth to the gate of the sun and let them fall in the fire to be with the king of devils and Death for ever.

The ETERNAL in the heaven of heavens with His Ark Angels was looking on earth to see Judgment by Elijah with the WORD, CHRIST and Zion sat on the throne, Zion said, Jerusalem come and seat next to me and your Father, Jesus and all his Brothers and Sisters sat around the throne looking on earth with multitudes of Angels in the Tabernacle and Angels who could not make it to the Tabernacle were watching on the network of the universe to see the Final judgment on devils to give CHRIST the Victory to rule the worlds in the Universe without godly spirits of the devils and Death.

Elijah commanded the chambers in Hades to open and also commanded the exit gate in the earth to open, there was a great rush by devils, godly spirits, rapists, pervert, murderers, thieves, false preachers, who scorned Elijah and CHRIST in religion, dictators and terrorists shedding blood on earth to destroy the Kingdom shouting freedom, freedom from the Lord he is merciful alleluia pushing and shoving saying hurry, hurry before the lord change his mind.

From the first sunrise the devils and godly spirits began to surface above from the deep waters the Spirit of the sun began to pull them up from the earth to the gate of the sun as fast as they were surfacing from the deep in Hades they were pulled up like a magnet pulling up dust and released they began to fall in the devouring fire in the sun fulfilling the prophesy of what CHRIST would do if the devils made a god and what Elijah would do to Devils and the strongest gods to send them all to Death.

Elijah thundered with the WORD to CHRIST and Zion this judgment is for bringing shame on you Jesus, Jerusalem and her Brothers and Sisters and killing Hebrews Judgment is justified to remove the devils and godly spirits for their sin on earth and eliminating holy people from earth. The Hebrews sang woe, woe, woe if spirits don't have faith in Elijah when CHRIST will come on the days of salvation to create Spirits.

The Angels began to clap hallelujah, Elijah, Elijah he has executed judgment on the devils and godly spirits for declaring war for the earth they began to clap and sing CHRIST and Zion, Reign with Excellence and Majesty by the WORD with Elijah, He has Judged and execute righteous Justice according to the prophesy of the ETERNAL for CHRIST AND ZION to rule on the throne in heaven.

Jerusalem sang Elijah I have seen your judgment in heaven now our children (Hebrews) will multiply in peace, Elijah thundered now I shall take a rest until the remnants in the nations populate and make multitudes of kingdoms for salvation from every tribe from your flesh for CHRIST to create Spirits in the Light so return to earth to be the Queen mother with Righteous Spirits of the Living in kingdoms from the flesh of Jerusalem in on earth. Elijah said now I shall take my rest until CHRIST return to create Spirits in Kingdoms for the final judgment on spirits that has no faith and Anti CHRIST. Elijah rested.(Rev 14.15:Ps97.1-12)

THE SUN ECLIPSE AND THERE WAS DARKNESS WHILE ELIJAH FELL ASLEEP

Elijah fell in a deep sleep, and suddenly the Spirit of the sun began to eclipse and the world was in darkness. CHRIST wanted to make everything new in the heavens, He released the comets and they began bombarding the old ancient planets of dark worlds and the worlds began to crack up and scatter boulders, and dust all over the worlds in the universe, some big stones fell on the earth as a remembrance and shook the earth.

The comets hit the ancient worlds in the dark until they were all destroyed so no worlds of devils remain in the universe for spirits of gods on earth to inhabit if they had no faith to do like the devils to want to make gods with Angels

The worlds was in darkness due to the dust and explosions an collision by comets destroying the remainder of the dark worlds, sunlight could not be seen, Elijah was in deep sleep, CHRIST called Elijah, Elijah wake up Elijah said its not time for salvation and went back in a deep sleep the Angels began to pray for Elijah to wake up to command the Spirit of the sun to let its light shine in the universe.

CHRIST called, Elijah, Elijah wake up the Spirit of the sun wait for you to say the WORD to pass judgment on the spirit of darkness for light to shine in the worlds, Elijah was in a deep sleep. CHRIST commanded the earth to tremble where Elijah was asleep, Elijah sprang up from sleep and saw the world was in darkness and heard spirits saying you can't bring judgment on us while the world is in darkness we still have sprits from the seed of the spirit of darkness on earth.

Elijah commanded the Spirit of the sun to let its light shine and let darkness be in the world until the end of spirits in kingdoms for salvation to fulfill the Testament of CHRIST to remove the spirits of gods in the flesh of Zion and Jerusalem and return those who has no

Faith to Death and the spirit of darkness, so all Spirits in the Light can live in the worlds in the Light without Darkness, Death, devils and godly spirits forever.

THE FALL OF DEVILS AND GODLY SPIRITS

Multitudes of Angels shouted Hallelujah, Hallelujah when the sun began to light the worlds and clap their hands and dance giving CHRIST praise for his wisdom creating His Elijah and gave him His plan to remove the devils from the Earth by the WORD to give Him the Victory over Death to fulfill the prophesy of the Eternal.

Jerusalem began clapping her hands singing Elijah bring on the final Eclipse to be your Queen the devils are finally captured, the Angels sang praise his holy name Elijah for doing holy work for peace and harmony in the worlds.

Death asked the king of devils in Hell who are these godly spirits wince come they that has joined us in this devouring fire they don't look like devils, where did they come from what evil have they done to be in fire with us? Satan said they belong to religious sects of devils from the earth and they were sent for tormenting holy people with false doctrine with the commandments of Death and for passing the seed of devils to make spirits for you Death.

A godly spirit cried to Death Satan came to earth with other devils and made us in the flesh of holy women to make gods his creation on earth and we are sent here in the fire to be with you for ever for murder, rape, stealing, killing holy people, kidnapping arson and passing on your disease to destroy holy flesh to be with Death.

Satan cried in fear of what the King of devils and Death would do him for fucking the mother of devils, he cried in fear it was in there nature to fuck their mother like you king with all your wickedness from Death, O king of devils they had a choice to obey like devils but they have the same passion like devils to make gods to fall in fire.

The King of devils said Satan before you and your revolution chained me to be king of the worlds I warned you would fall for fucking your mother, she was never satisfied and wanted to make a creature better than me now they are cast out of the earth and are in fire crying.

The king of devils said if you were not a mother fucker you would not have so many godly spirits in hell crying for water and flesh to eat in this heat for eternity, because of you and your mother wanting to make something better than devils from Death all your hard work has come to nothing and make the ETERNAL and HIS CHRIST and Elijah and all Angels laugh at Death and devils as the scum of the universe and your gods you left on earth are making a fool of you making kingdoms for Salvation for CHRIST to create Spirits in the Light.

THE VICTORY OVER DEATH

The king of devils said: Satan Elijah has sent all of you from the Earth to give CHRIST the Victory over Death, because you made a god on earth we loss all our worlds from ancient times from the spirit of darkness for CHRIST and ZION Reign for eternity nm

SALVATION IS THE END OF SPIRITS OF GODS ON THE EARTH

In the beginning the ETERNAL prophesied what CHRIST will do when he and Zion sit on the throne in heaven and what Elijah will do if the devil made a god with his creation to make the statutes with the devils obsolete for all Spirits in the light to live by the new testament of CHRIST.

No Angel knew who is CHRIST or Zion or which world they would come from all the Angels Knew the two seats on the Throne in heaven was for Christ and Zion and when they sat on the throne CHRIST will be a creator and will rule and have dominion in all worlds in the universe.

The ETERNAL Spirit in the Light prophesied the devils would make a god and the god would end in the deep for disobedience.

The ETERNAL prophesied the earth will be populated with spirits of gods in the kingdom.

The ETERNAL prophesied Sprits of CHRIST will populate Sprits in the Light in kingdoms on earth among spirits of gods and devils and the spirits of gods will multiply on earth abundantly.

The ETERNAL prophesied the devils and godly spirits would be gathered in a place they have not been and Christ would let the spirits of gods in the kingdom to live on earth for seasons and days and the Hour of salvation for CHRIST to create Spirits the kingdom of gods to populate the earth with Sprits in the Light.

Salvation is the end of spirits of gods in the kingdom and the spirits of gods that has no faith in Elijah will be sent in the fire. The spirits of gods that has faith will prepare their kingdom to have a Sprit in the Light on the days of salvation

The godly spirits of Judah had knowledge of salvation and knew Elijah is the Judge of the earth, when He released the godly spirits from Hades they possessed the body with spirits of gods and indoctrinate the spirits in their religion to lose faith for peace.

Jn.8.34-34 In the time of Jesus he said to a godly spirits in the body of a Jew you a god of your father the son of the devil and you wish to do the desire of god your father. A godly spirit said through the mouth of a Jew the Law command we worship God of god of our father the flesh of our Mother is for an offering for salvation. Satan gave Judah hope after death he disobeyed Elijah who offered him eternal peace.

Jesus told Israel on the mountain there is none on earth that is great as Elijah, the scripture is all about what Elijah will do, and he had a choice to learn from Elijah so his body could have a Sprit created to be his Son in the Light.

Israel said we gave up everything to follow you thinking there was hope when we returned from captivity. Jesus replied but you shall receive multitudes of godly spiritshas no faith like you on the days of salvation the fathers of your children that was saved in the flood told their children to tell their children to have faith in Elijah he is a king with Jerusalem

THE SECRET

AMMON alias name Judah spirit name Israel was brought up by Elijah. Elijah gave him a choice to have eternal peace for salvation of his body to create a Sprit in the Light to be his Son. Judah put his hope with the devils to be a king of the earth and kept salvation as his secret, salvation was not understood by gods to know the choice for peace but instead worshiped him as the mighty God with the mysteries of life so all on earth would not know the power of Elijah to save them from Death in the consuming fire.

Because Judah was not accepted above he became a jealous god with hate for Elijah and Christ and put fear in all mankind if they did not worship him as the mighty God they would fall to Death. Elijah has a better plan for all mankind to have faith in him to have eternal peace instead of fire in hell. The choice is for all spirits of gods to decide their fate while they live in the kingdom before CHRIST come to create Spirits.

Death was kept a secret by the godly spirits that returned from captivity in Hades and made mankind to think a dead body was unto Death. Death is a spirit from the Element of darkness a sinner with all kinds of disease nothing about Death should be kept a secret and all should be told of the choice to have faith for eternal peace

The problem facing spirits of gods in the kingdom is having no know knowledge what their future will be after they are dead, not knowing who they are or there connection with Death, not knowing what is required for everlasting peace when they are no more human or denial of their spirituality and want to force their way to heaven like the almighty God, not knowing who can save them from Death, not knowing CHRIST is not Jesus and Elijah is More than a prophet so there is much confusion and leading astray with no hope and not knowing who to have faith in to save them.

The godly spirits of the dead had authority over the spirit in there humanity. Jesus warned mankind and Jews the godly spirits could see through their eyes and hear through their ears but they could not understand Jesus was sent by CHRIST to tell them the truth about salvation and Peace and to stop following false doctrines that lead to Death. Those Jesus spoke who were not spirits in the light said he spoke in Parables.

When Jesus was among Hebrews who are Spirits in the light in the kingdom he told them they can pray directly to Christ in heaven our Farther is in heaven they are Spirits in the Light populating the earth according to the prophecy of the Eternal. But for spirits of gods they have to go through Elijah to have peace, if they have faith in ELIJAH he will save them from Death, spirits of gods are not accepted in heaven and should go about their daily lives putting their life in the hands of Elijah the Son of CHRIST by the WORD and with the WORD,mankind and Jews an indoctrinated with worshiping gods in their nation.

THE BEGINNING OF THE END

The ETERNAL Spirit in the Light prophesied before he created CHRIST and Zion to the Angels what CHRIST will do when He sit on the throne with Zion and what Elijah will do to fulfill His prophecy to make the statues with the devils obsolete for all Angels and Spirits CHRIST created in the Light to live by the new Testament of CHRIST

No Angel knew who is Christ or Zion or which world they would come from, all they knew when CHRIST took office he will be a creator of Spirits in the Light when Zion sit on the Throne with Him to rule all worlds in the universe

The ETERNAL prophesied CHRIST and Zion will be in the Light and have Spirits in the Light. The ETERNAL prophesied the devil will make a god an god will end in the deep, He prophesied the devils will populate the earth with gods and CHRIST will let the spirits of gods multiply abundantly to make kingdoms for Christ to create to Spirits to live in heavens

The Eternal prophesied Elijah would gather the devils together and send them to a place they have never been with there godly spirits for a time to let the spirits of gods on earth populate and multiply abundantly to make Kingdoms for salvation for CHRIST to create Spirits in the Light in abundance to live in heavens, (15:20)

The work of Creation in the Kingdoms for salvation is between CHRIST and Elijah until salvation End with no more spirits of gods are on earth. Judgment on spirits of gods is between Elijah and the Spirit of the sun after Christ create Spirits and on his return to heaven bring up the spirits that awake from sleep on Earth to heaven and take His rest for 6 days.

The Judgment by the Spirit of the sun is automatic to pull up every spirit of gods that has no rest from nation to nation sun rise to sun set to the gate of the Sun to fall in the fire to be with devils and Death, and rest on the 7th Day. It is a fearful thing not to have faith in Elijah to sleep for Eternity.

Everything that is hid shall be known and nothing should be kept a secret and should tell their friends and family the way to Death is for many who has no faith in Elijah. Jesus told the people that followed him, your forefathers that was saved in the vessel in the flood, Elijah told them to tell their children to tell their children to have faith in him to save them. ELIJAH is the King with Jerusalem.

A godly sprit said that returned from captivity told Jesus we gave up everything to follow you thinking there is hope. Jesus replied you don't have faith you shall be among the multitudes that has no faith in salvation, the harvest of kingdoms is the end of spirits of gods and the spirits that has no faith will end in fire, except you see signs you will not believe and want to keep the doctrine of God he thought he was wise man and perished for hiding the Knowledge of Elijah he had no Faith.

A god said Jesus the Law of God of our father say we should worship him but the flesh of our mother is an offering to do holy work. Jesus said there is none greater than Elijah for it is Him the scripture is about, learn from me have faith in Elijah and you shall have Eternal peace.

THE END of spirits of gods on earth

According to the prophesy of the ETERNAL Chapter 15: 20 let the spirits of gods in the Kingdoms Populate the earth with spirits CHRIST will let the spirits of gods multiply abundantly to make kingdoms for CHRIST to create SPIRITS in the LIGHT in abundance to live in the Heavens

Salvation is the End of spirits of gods in the Kingdom to make way for Spirits in the Light, gods should be observant of the signs and believe the End is quick.

The south wind will blow hot air on the ice in the north to melt the ice and return to the Ice in the south and the ice will melt, as the ice melts the earth get hot and cause a lot of draught. The days of salvation clouds in the nations and rain and floods, tempests blowing and circulating the heat for bush fires and earth quakes and mountainous waves returning to its sea level before the Flood. The ice is like an egg timer as a warning sign to the end. Let gods be for seasons and years and days and the hour to End Salvation in Kingdoms to be as it was in the Beginning with CHRIST and ZION by the WORD with no god on earth.

After Salvation the Sun will eclipse and darkness will be no more in the universe the whole Universe will be in the Light with Angels Living under the Testament of Christ.

THE PROPHECY OF THE END

THE FINAL TESTAMENT OF GOD OF THE DEVIL AND GOD HIS SON

Ro7.8 god of the devil confessed to the Romans he is from the devil, in sin Eve concieved him. all gods are born in sin and any god that blaspheme CHRIST shall not be forgivev in this world foreever.

R0.7.8 god said through the mouth of Paul any god who speak against Elijah is ignorant.

Deut 27.22 god said through the mouth of Paul cursed is God his son, he lieth with his mother who I raped and she concieved him

Deut 27.20 god said cursed is the devil who raped Eve to make a god. Cursed is the devil who kidnaped the daughter of CHRIST to make gods while she was pregnant for me the first god of the devil.

EPH 1.23 god said through the mouth of Judas: God was made a prince by satan, then made him a king with the devils while they were on earth

Deut. 21.15; god said the first god born of the daughter of CHRIST is my god through rape for her to make a god to look like me.

!Pet.4 11--15 Godly spirit wrote through the hand of Peter Dear friends do not be surprised as what I write will surprise you, it is because of me you are suffering, I am a murderer. it is who Killed the the SONS of CHRIST/ADAM and elimated them from the earth, I am a criminal sheding blood on the earth to be a king with the devils.

!Pet.4.16-17 Godly spirit of God, wrote through the hand of Peter I am ashamed and plead with Elijah to save you from hell, I am afraid of the outcome for the spirits from my seed that has no Faith in Elijah to save you. This is the TRUTH

! Pet.4.18-19 Godly spirit of God wrote thhrough the hand of Peter: It was hard for me to belive in Salvation by Elijah. now I am a godlly spirit released from captivity, I sinned with my mother so prepare your body for Salvation and have FAITH in Elijah so your body can becreated with a new SPIRIT to continue while your sprit rest in Peace.

! Pet. 5.1,10 God wrote through the hand of Peter: I am a godly spirit released from captivity to Testify I executed judgment on CHRIST while He was the SPIRIT in Adam. Godly of god wrote through the hand of Peter it is I who hanged the body of CHRIST on a tree , I am your enemy, I have decieved you, Iam a hypocrete and want the same suffering for all godly spirits from my seed.

Elijah released me and other godlly spirits to seduce the spirits in there humanity the way to eternal Life. Elijah has Authority and Power over all godlly spirits for ever, While you are human have FAITH in Elijah. AMEN.

! Pet. 5.13 God wrote through the hand of Peter: I was the King with my mother in Babylon, I made her my Queen. She is now a SPIRIT,her SPIRIT name is Jerusalem all spirits of gods are in her flesh.Her flesh is her inheritance for CHRIST to create SPIRITS when the Earth is populated with multitudes of gods. through Elijah to have to have everlasting Life

2 Pet. 2.10 God wrote through the hand of Peter before returning to captivity : godly spirits in there humanity has no Knowledge while they live in there humanity. Elijah has released me from captivity in hell to enter bodies to seduce the spirits of gods to prepare there body for Salvation, so there spirits rest in Peace after CHRIST cast out godly spirits from the flesh of his daughter Jerusalem , so He can create New Spirits to manifest in his daughters flesh to have Knowledge

2 Pet. 2.12 God wrote through the hand of Peter before returning to mcaptivity: As long as I am allowed to be in the body of Peter, I will want you my mother, I know I must depart from this body. Elijah has made it clear to me I must return to hell. My mother I will make every effort to see you before my departure.

2 Pet. 1.17; 21 God wrote through the hand of Peter his last testament: I was the one who hanged Adam with my soldiers as my witness. I did not see CHRIST SPIRIT when He departed from the body of Adam as I was I was still human, I was a prophet to gods of the devils teaching them the Law of devils to live to Death. Idid not belive Elijah was a HOLY SPIRT until I was carried away in captivity, my spirit was without flesh.

2 Pet. 2. 1 God wrote through the hand of Peter before returning to Captivity :I am false and ministered the law of devils, I took the oath

of devils to hate Elijah and CHRIST, While I was a godly spirit in my humanity I followed the devils way

Eph 1.23 While the devils was on Earth.Satan made him a Prince, then made God a King with the devils

Rom 7.8 Any god who speak against Elijah and CHRIST isignorant.

www.ingramcontent.com/pod-product-compliance
Lightning Source LLC
Chambersburg PA
CBHW021618120626
46545CB00001B/281